I0499996

Indonesia
Cultural Awareness and
Business Negotiations

Country Study

Contents

INTRODUCTION

In our increasingly interconnected world, understanding and embracing cultural diversity has become essential for both personal and professional success. This series of Cultural Awareness books aims to provide participants with the knowledge, skills, and tools necessary to better understand and navigate various cultural contexts. By investing in cultural awareness, we are not only fostering stronger relationships but also paving the way for more successful business ventures and personal growth.

The expanding Global market presents immense opportunities for businesses. However, these opportunities come with the responsibility of understanding the nuances of various cultures. Unintentional cultural misunderstandings can jeopardise your chances of securing a crucial foothold in this lucrative market. This series highlights the importance of being aware of cultural differences and equips you with the tools to deal with the challenges that may arise when interacting with individuals from different cultural backgrounds.

Individuals and families who have travelled or are planning to move to different countries also face the challenge of adapting to new cultures. Culture shock can be overwhelming if one is not prepared to handle the changes that come with relocating. This course offers practical insights and tools to help individuals and families better understand and navigate the complexities of their new cultural environment.

Cultural awareness goes beyond learning facts or memorizing customs; it is about cultivating a genuine appreciation for the richness of human experiences. This series encourages participants to look beyond their own cultural lens and develop empathy for the perspectives of others. By doing so, we foster a more inclusive and harmonious world where people from diverse backgrounds can come together and create meaningful connections.

Throughout this book, you will be introduced to various cultural frameworks, practices, and traditions, as well as common misconceptions and stereotypes that often contribute to misunderstandings and miscommunications. Engaging with these topics will enable you to recognise cultural differences, appreciate their value, and navigate them effectively.

In conclusion, cultural awareness is essential for anyone aiming to expand their reach in the global market, adapt to new cultural environments, or enrich their lives by embracing the beauty of human diversity. By undertaking this journey, you are taking a significant step toward creating a more inclusive, empathetic, and successful future.

Ask yourself: Can you afford to miss out on the vital opportunities and personal growth that cultural awareness can bring to your life? The time to invest in cultural understanding is now. Welcome to an enlightening and transformative journey.

1. WHAT IS CULTURE?

What is Culture?

The Culture of a people can be understood as the system of shared ideas and meanings, explicit and implicit, which a people use to interpret the world and which serve to pattern their behaviour.

This includes an understanding of the art, literature, and history of a society, but also less tangible aspects such as attitudes, prejudices, folklore etc. Unconscious or conscious habits are just as important as art and history.

<u>Values</u> - What people say one ought to do or not do? What is considered good or bad - the importance of honesty, or chastity?

<u>Laws</u> - What political authorities have decided people should do, and what the sanctions are?

<u>Rules</u> - What a society has decided its members should do. Social rules about marriage ages, childrearing.

<u>Social Categories</u>- Ways of thinking about people as types. - "friends", "criminals", "lovers", "nobles", "clergy".

<u>Tacit Models</u> - Implicit standards and patterns of behaviour that a person does not think about - knowing how to address a police officer rather than friends. Knowing how to dress for a job interview as opposed to a dance.

<u>Fundamental</u> - Categories and ways of thinking that people take for granted and may not recognise even when pointed out. - thinking in dualities good/bad, male/female.

Culture shapes

- The way we think
- The way we interact
- The way we communicate
- The way we transmit knowledge to the next generation

Culture manifests itself in

- Food
- Religion
- Dress
- Differences in language
- Our expectations of male and female roles
- Non-verbal rules and body language

The first step is in understanding the values and rules for behaviour of our own culture - the "normal" or "right" way of doing things. What makes us different?

Geert Hofstede

Between 1967 and 1973 Geert Hofstede conducted a study on culture across 100 000 employees of IBM in 50 countries. From this he developed a framework to 'measure' the 'value dimensions' of various cultures.

Hofstede identified 4 values which can be related to each culture:

- Individualism
- Masculinity
- Power Distance, and
- Uncertainty Avoidance

Later studies by Trompenaar have added several more; however, I will address the 4 basic values along with one later addition relating to time.

From surveys, Hofstede was able to map the cultures and compare them, and from this extrapolate as to why a culture may act in a particular way.

Taking the basic values separately, measured on a scale of 0 to 100;

	PD	ID	M	UA	LT
ID	78H	14L	46L	48L	62H
AUS	38L	90H	61H	51M	21L
USA	40	91	62	46	26
UK	35	89	66	35	51

H = top third of countries
M = medium
L = bottom third

Power Distance

In this dimension, we explore the concept that not all individuals within societies are equal, reflecting the culture's attitude towards these disparities. Power Distance is defined as the degree to which less powerful members of institutions and organizations within a country anticipate and accept that power is distributed unevenly.

In Indonesia, there is a high emphasis on power distance (with a score of **78**), which is characterized by a strong reliance on hierarchy, unequal rights between those with and without power, limited accessibility to superiors, directive leadership, and centralized control. Managers expect obedience from their team members, while employees anticipate clear instructions on their tasks. Respect for authority is vital, and communication tends to be indirect, with negative feedback being concealed. The high power distance in Indonesia also results in a significant guru-student dynamic, where colleagues expect clear guidance from their superiors. Westerners may be taken aback by the visible and socially accepted vast disparity between the rich and poor in the country.

Individualism v. Collectivism

This dimension addresses the level of interdependence that a society maintains among its members, focusing on whether individuals perceive themselves in terms of "I" or "We." In individualistic societies, people are expected to take care of themselves and their immediate family members only. In collectivist societies, individuals belong to 'in-groups' (such as families, clans, or organizations) that provide care and support in exchange for loyalty.

In Indonesia, a collectivist society with a low score of **14**, there is a strong emphasis on adhering to a well-defined social framework where individuals conform to societal ideals and their respective in-groups. This collectivist culture is particularly evident in family dynamics and relationships.

For instance, when it comes to marriage, it is crucial for a man to meet a woman's family, as family plays a vital role in her life. To be taken seriously by a woman, a man must formally introduce himself to her parents. Courting a woman without informing her parents first is considered inappropriate.

Another example of Indonesia's collectivist culture is the deep bond between children and their parents. Indonesian children are devoted to their parents throughout their lives, striving to ease their parents' burdens and support them in their old age. A widely accepted saying in Indonesia is, "You can get another wife or husband but not another mother or father." This strong family loyalty is also demonstrated by Indonesian families caring for their elderly relatives, such as grandparents, at home instead of placing them in institutions. In contrast, individualist societies typically prioritize the nuclear family unit.

Masculinity v. Femininity

A high score (Masculine) on this dimension signifies that a society is driven by competition, achievement, and success, where success is defined by being the winner or the best in one's field. This value system starts in school and continues throughout organizational life.

A low score (Feminine) on this dimension indicates that the dominant values in society prioritize caring for others and quality of life. In a Feminine society, quality of life is considered a sign of success, and standing out from the crowd is not admired. The fundamental issue here is what motivates people: wanting to be the best (Masculine) or enjoying what they do (Feminine).

Indonesia has a score of **46** on the masculinity dimension, making it a low masculine society. Although not as feminine as some North European countries, it is less masculine compared to other Asian countries like Japan, China, and India. In Indonesia, status and visible symbols of success are essential, but material gain is not always the primary motivator. Instead, a person's position may hold more significance due to the Indonesian concept of "gengsi," which loosely translates to "outward appearances." Maintaining a strong "gengsi" is crucial in projecting an impressive image and creating an aura of status.

In feminine countries, the focus is on "working to live," where managers seek consensus, and people prioritize equality, solidarity, and quality in their work lives. Conflicts are resolved through compromise and negotiation, with incentives such as free time and flexibility being favoured. The emphasis is on well-being, and status is not flaunted. An effective manager is a supportive one, and decision-making involves participation. In contrast, low masculine countries, which are not feminine enough to be classified as feminine societies, exhibit masculine traits but to a lesser degree.

Uncertainty Avoidance

The Uncertainty Avoidance dimension addresses how societies cope with the fact that the future is always uncertain: should we attempt to control the future or simply let it unfold? The inherent ambiguity in the future creates anxiety, and different cultures have developed various ways to manage this anxiety. The extent to which a culture's members feel threatened by ambiguous or unknown situations and have established beliefs and institutions to mitigate these uncertainties is reflected in their Uncertainty Avoidance score.

Indonesia scores **48** on the uncertainty avoidance dimension, indicating a low preference for avoiding uncertainty. This preference is reflected in the Javanese cultural practice of separating one's internal self from their external self. When upset, Indonesians tend not to display negative emotions or anger outwardly, maintaining a polite demeanour and smile despite their internal feelings. This behaviour also emphasizes the importance of workplace and relationship harmony, as individuals avoid being the bearers of negative news or feedback.

In conflict resolution, Indonesians often find direct communication threatening and uncomfortable. A more successful and familiar approach is to use a third-party intermediary, which allows for the exchange of opinions without losing face and helps maintain workplace harmony by avoiding direct confrontation.

A key phrase that illustrates this concept in Indonesia is "Asal Bapak Senang" (Keep the Boss Happy). The rationale behind this phrase is multifaceted, but when considered in the context of uncertainty avoidance, keeping the boss happy leads to rewards, reduced economic and status uncertainty, and continued value within the company.

Long Term Orientation

With a high score of **62**, Indonesia demonstrates a pragmatic culture. In such societies, people believe that truth is heavily influenced by the situation, context, and time. They exhibit a strong capacity for adapting traditions to changing circumstances, a significant inclination to save and invest, frugality, and determination in achieving desired outcomes.

Acculturation

Acculturation is the process of adapting to a new culture.

- Variables affecting Acculturation
- The amount of time spent in the process – educating yourself
- The quantity and quality of interaction – trying things
- Ethnicity or nation of origin – how far is it removed from our own
- Affinity – willingness to learn and adapt

Stages of Acculturation

- Acceptance of new culture - honeymoon
- Individual starts to feel comfortable in the new culture
- Feelings of anger, hostility, and frustration
- Recovery
- Culture Shock

Generalisations

We should remember that there will probably never be one person within a culture that actually meets these dimensions. Rather this is a tool to anticipate likely reaction of a particular culture. There is never an average person! What should be remembered is that between the extremes, patterns do exist.

The inverse also applies; do not confuse a particular individual's personality as representative of culture. Whilst Australian's are considered sports loving people, there are people who don't like Rugby – as hard as that is to believe!

Stereotyping – setting a standard idea, concept or form. This 'notion' has a deeper meaning to our basic survival instincts.

Bias – a particular tendency or preference, which may prevent unprejudiced consideration of a topic. A 'learned' response.

Prejudice - an unfavourable opinion formed beforehand or without knowledge or reason.

Linear and Circular Thinking

How does culture affect Management?

Our Western (Greek) method of teaching & learning is if there is a problem then I can solve it. We are taught to identify issues as a 'problem' that challenges us. The individual works out a plan and overcomes the problem.

In a culture not rooted in the Western traditions, the issue may not be seen as a 'problem'!! Rather it is a divergence or even a side issue that can be avoided or not confronted until a solution is evident

Managing Across Culture

The management theory of MBI (Mapping – Bridging – Integrating) was developed to understand the differences and work out optimum paths to achieve greater work flows.

2. INTRODUCTION

The Importance of Cultural Awareness for Families and Business

In today's increasingly interconnected world, understanding and embracing different cultures is essential for both personal and professional success. With the advent of globalization and the ease of international travel, families and businesses alike find themselves navigating new cultural landscapes. For those moving to or conducting business in another country, cultivating cultural awareness is crucial to ensure a smooth transition and build lasting relationships in this vibrant country.

For families relocating, cultural awareness is the key to integrating successfully into their new home. By understanding the customs, values, and social norms of a society, families can better adapt to their surroundings and foster meaningful connections with their new neighbours. Familiarizing oneself with the language, local etiquette, and traditions can help ease the challenges of adjusting to a new environment, allowing families to fully immerse themselves in the rich cultural tapestry of a new country.

In the realm of business, cultural awareness is equally important. As countries continue to grow as economic powers, many international companies and entrepreneurs are seizing opportunities in the dynamic markets. Mastering the intricacies of business culture can help professionals negotiate deals effectively, avoid misunderstandings, and forge strong partnerships with their counterparts. By respecting local customs and demonstrating cultural sensitivity, businesspeople can build trust and credibility, essential ingredients for success in any international venture.

This comprehensive guide aims to equip families and professionals with the knowledge and tools necessary to embrace a foreign culture and thrive in their personal and professional lives. Through an exploration of history, values, and social norms, readers will gain valuable insights into the intricacies of a society. Additionally, practical advice on navigating daily life, social interactions, and business negotiations will empower families and professionals alike to make the most of their time in this captivating country.

As you embark on your journey, remember that cultural awareness is an ongoing process, requiring patience, openness, and a willingness to learn. By embracing the unique qualities that make a different culture such a fascinating place to live and work, you can create lasting memories, foster meaningful relationships, and unlock the full potential of your experience in this remarkable country.

The Importance of Understanding Indonesian Culture

Indonesia, an archipelago country located in Southeast Asia, is the world's fourth most populous nation, with over 270 million people belonging to more than 300 ethnic groups. With such a diverse population, understanding Indonesian culture becomes essential for several reasons, including fostering better communication, promoting mutual respect, and enhancing business and social relationships. Here, we will delve into some of the most significant reasons why understanding Indonesian culture is important.

Enhancing communication and relationships

Understanding the language, customs, and values of Indonesian culture enables more effective communication with the locals, leading to stronger personal and professional relationships. Indonesia has its official language, Bahasa Indonesia, but over 700 different languages and dialects are spoken throughout the country. By learning the language and understanding the culture, one can better appreciate the nuances of interpersonal communication in Indonesia.

Fostering mutual respect

Indonesia is a melting pot of various religions, customs, and traditions. Respecting and understanding these differences is crucial for promoting tolerance and reducing potential conflicts. For example, the majority of Indonesians are Muslims, and acknowledging their religious practices and beliefs will contribute to a harmonious relationship.

Business opportunities

As the largest economy in Southeast Asia, Indonesia offers numerous business opportunities for both local and foreign investors. Understanding Indonesian business culture, which values relationships and trust, is vital for successful partnerships and negotiations. Recognizing the importance of "saving face" and respecting the hierarchical nature of Indonesian society will also help facilitate smoother business transactions.

Strengthening tourism

Indonesia is renowned for its breathtaking landscapes, rich culture, and warm hospitality. Understanding and appreciating the customs, traditions, and beliefs of the Indonesian people can significantly enhance the tourist experience, leading to increased satisfaction and a higher likelihood of repeat visits.

Promoting cultural exchange

Indonesia's diverse culture can provide valuable insights and perspectives on various aspects of life, including art, cuisine, religion, and history. By understanding and appreciating this rich cultural heritage, individuals from different backgrounds can engage in meaningful cultural exchanges that promote understanding and respect.

Expanding global awareness: Learning about Indonesian culture is essential for individuals and organizations looking to expand their global awareness and understanding. As a member of several international organizations, such as the United Nations, the World Trade Organization, and the Association of Southeast Asian Nations (ASEAN), Indonesia plays a critical role in shaping global policies and initiatives.

3. UNDERSTANDING INDONESIAN CULTURE

A Brief History of Indonesia

To better understand Indonesian culture, it is essential to know its rich history that has shaped the nation's diverse customs and traditions. Here is a brief overview of the key events and periods in Indonesian history:

Early history (pre-4th century)

Indonesia, the largest archipelago on Earth, stretches over 5,000 kilometres from east to west, encompassing more than 17,000 islands. Its strategic location between Asia and Australia has led to a long and complex history, with diverse groups of people settling the islands throughout the millennia. The early history of Indonesia (pre-4th century) is marked by various waves of migration, which significantly influenced the formation of the country's culture and identity.

The earliest evidence of human occupation in Indonesia dates back to around 1.5 million years ago, when Homo erectus, known as "**Java Man**," roamed the islands. The remains of these early hominids were discovered near the Solo River in Java in the late 19th century. These early inhabitants were hunters and gatherers, relying on the abundant natural resources of the islands for sustenance.

Over the millennia, the Indonesian archipelago experienced multiple waves of migration from different parts of mainland Asia. The first wave of migration, known as the Austroasiatic migration, occurred around 4,000-3,000 BCE. These people brought with them new agricultural techniques, including the cultivation of rice and domestication of animals like chickens and pigs. They also introduced early forms of metallurgy, including the use of bronze for making tools and weapons.

The second wave of migration, known as the Austronesian migration, took place around 2,500-1,500 BCE. Originating from Taiwan, these people migrated southwards through the Philippines and into the Indonesian archipelago. They were skilled seafarers, navigating the vast expanses of the Pacific and Indian Oceans in their outrigger canoes.

The Austronesians introduced several significant cultural practices and technologies to Indonesia, including pottery making, loom weaving, and the construction of megalithic structures. They also introduced new agricultural techniques, such as the cultivation of root crops and tree crops like bananas and coconuts. The Austronesians were particularly skilled at navigating the seas, and their outrigger canoes allowed them to explore and colonize the vast Pacific and Indian Oceans.

During this early period, various groups of people on the Indonesian islands developed distinct cultural practices and languages. The islands of Sumatra, Java, and Borneo, for example, saw the development of complex irrigation systems for rice cultivation, while the people of the eastern islands relied more on fishing and maritime trade.

The pre-4th century history of Indonesia was also marked by the emergence of early regional polities, such as the Dvipantara and the **Kutai** Kingdom in East Kalimantan. These early kingdoms were characterized by a loose, decentralized structure, with regional rulers paying tribute to more powerful leaders.

Religion also played a significant role in the early history of Indonesia, with **animism** and ancestor worship being prevalent. The people believed in a wide array of spirits and supernatural beings, which inhabited the natural world and influenced their daily lives. Rituals, ceremonies, and offerings were made to appease these spirits and ensure a harmonious relationship between the human and spiritual worlds.

Hindu-Buddhist period (4th - 13th century)

The Hindu-Buddhist period in Indonesia, spanning from the 4th to the 13th century, marked a significant cultural transformation in the region. During this era, Indian influences reached the archipelago through trade, religious missions, and the spread of Indianised kingdoms. The fusion of indigenous and Indian cultural elements led to the creation of a unique civilization, characterized by the emergence of powerful Hindu-Buddhist empires, monumental architecture, and the development of sophisticated artistic and literary traditions.

The Indian influence in Indonesia began with the arrival of Indian merchants and **Brahmin scholars**, who introduced Hinduism and Buddhism to the region. The local rulers were particularly drawn to these new religions as they provided a sophisticated religious framework and a system of political legitimacy, based on the divine right of kings. The adoption of **Hinduism** and **Buddhism** also facilitated trade and cultural exchange with the Indian subcontinent, further strengthening the position of Indonesian kingdoms in the region.

Several significant Hindu-Buddhist empires emerged in Indonesia during this period, including the **Tarumanagara**, **Srivijaya**, and **Mataram** kingdoms. The Tarumanagara kingdom, which existed from the 4th to the 7th century, was one of the earliest Indianised kingdoms in Indonesia, centred in present-day West Java. The kingdom's rulers adopted Hinduism and patronized the construction of Hindu temples, including the **Cangkuang** temple in Garut.

The Srivijaya empire, which flourished from the 7th to the 13th century, was a powerful maritime and trading empire based in present-day Palembang, Sumatra. Srivijaya exerted significant influence over the Strait of Malacca, the Sunda Strait, and the coastal areas of Sumatra, Java, and the Malay Peninsula. The empire was a centre of Buddhist learning, attracting scholars and pilgrims from across the Buddhist world, including the famous Chinese monk Yijing. The Srivijaya empire's wealth and power were derived from its control over the lucrative spice trade and its strategic location along the maritime Silk Road.

The Mataram kingdom, which existed from the 8th to the 10th century, was a powerful Javanese Hindu-Buddhist empire that controlled much of central and eastern Java. The kingdom's rulers were known for their patronage of monumental architecture, including the construction of the spectacular Borobudur and Prambanan temple complexes. Borobudur, a 9th-century Mahayana Buddhist temple, is the world's largest Buddhist monument, while Prambanan, a 9th-century Hindu temple complex, is one of the largest and most beautiful Hindu temple complexes in Southeast Asia.

Art and literature flourished during the Hindu-Buddhist period, with the development of classical Javanese literature, such as the Ramayana and the Mahabharata, which were translated and adapted from the Indian epics. The period also saw the creation of original Javanese literary works, such as the Arjunawiwaha and the Kakawin Sutasoma. In addition to literature, the period witnessed the development of a rich tradition of visual and performing arts, including sculpture, painting, dance, and wayang (shadow puppetry).

The Age of Islam (13th - 16th century)

The Age of Islam in Indonesia, spanning from the 13th to the 16th century, marked a significant turning point in the nation's history. During this period, Islam emerged as the dominant religion in the archipelago, gradually displacing Hinduism and Buddhism. This era witnessed the rise of influential Islamic sultanates, the dissemination of Islamic art and culture, and the eventual fusion of Islamic and indigenous Indonesian beliefs and practices.

The introduction of Islam to Indonesia is primarily attributed to Muslim traders from the Arabian Peninsula, Persia, and India. These merchants established trading posts along the coastal regions of Sumatra, Java, and the Malay Peninsula, bringing not only goods but also their religious beliefs. The egalitarian nature of Islam, its focus on trade, and the extensive network of Muslim trading communities that extended from East Africa to China made it appealing to the region's rulers and coastal elites. Consequently, they embraced Islam, enticed by the prospect of increased trade and diplomatic relations with the broader Islamic world.

One of the earliest Islamic sultanates in the region was the Sultanate of Samudra Pasai, which emerged in the 13th century in present-day Aceh, Sumatra. Samudra Pasai became a vital centre for the spread of Islam, thanks to its strategic location along the Strait of Malacca and its role as a hub for regional trade. In Central Java, the Sultanate of Demak, established in the 14th century, played a crucial role in the Islamization of Java and its neighbouring islands. The Sultanate of Malacca, founded in the early 15th century, also significantly contributed to the spread of Islam in the region due to its importance as a centre of trade and diplomacy.

As Islam spread throughout the Indonesian archipelago, it interacted with local customs and beliefs, resulting in a unique form of Islam characterized by distinct Indonesian features. This form of Islam, often referred to as "syncretic" or "indigenous Islam," incorporated elements of pre-Islamic Indonesian culture, such as animism and ancestor worship. This syncretism facilitated Islam's acceptance by the local population and its integration into the fabric of Indonesian society.

The Age of Islam also saw the development of Islamic art, architecture, and literature in Indonesia. Islamic art's influence is evident in the intricate wood carvings, calligraphy, and geometric patterns that adorn mosques, palaces, and other public buildings. Islamic architecture in Indonesia reflects a fusion of local building traditions and Islamic design principles, as evidenced by the multi-tiered roofs and slender minarets of Indonesian mosques. The period also witnessed the flourishing of Islamic literature, with the creation of original works in the Malay and Javanese languages, such as the **Hikayat Raja-Raja Pasai** and the **Serat Centhini**.

The spread of Islam in Indonesia had significant political implications as well. The emergence of Islamic sultanates and the adoption of Islamic political systems reinforced the centralization of power and the establishment of more structured and hierarchical societies. This development paved the way for the rise of powerful Islamic empires, such as the Aceh Sultanate and the Mataram Sultanate, which would come to dominate the political landscape of Indonesia in the centuries that followed.

European colonisation (16th - 20th century)

European colonization of Indonesia began in the early 16th century and continued until the mid-20th century, profoundly impacting the political, economic, and social landscape of the archipelago. During this period, European powers such as the Portuguese, Dutch, and British vied for control over the valuable resources and strategic trade routes in the region. The Dutch, however, would ultimately emerge as the dominant colonial power, establishing a centuries-long rule over the Indonesian archipelago.

The Portuguese were the first Europeans to arrive in Indonesia, driven by their quest for valuable spices and the desire to establish a foothold in the lucrative Asian trade network. In 1511, the Portuguese captured Malacca, a major trading hub on the Malay Peninsula, and soon began forging alliances with local rulers in the Moluccas (Spice Islands). They established a number of forts and trading posts throughout the archipelago, securing their control over the valuable clove and nutmeg trade.

However, the Portuguese monopoly on the spice trade was short-lived, as the Dutch and British soon entered the fray. The **Dutch East India Company** (VOC), founded in 1602, aggressively pursued its interests in the region, establishing a network of trading posts and exerting control over local rulers. By the mid-17th century, the Dutch had effectively ousted the

Portuguese from the Indonesian archipelago and gained control over the lucrative spice trade. The British, on the other hand, focused their efforts on establishing trading posts in Bencoolen (present-day Bengkulu) and other parts of Sumatra, but their influence in the region was largely overshadowed by the Dutch.

The VOC's rule over Indonesia was characterized by ruthless exploitation of resources and brutal suppression of local resistance. The Dutch imposed a monopoly on the production and trade of valuable commodities, such as spices, coffee, and sugar, forcing local farmers to cultivate cash crops for the Dutch market under the "**cultivation system**." This exploitative system led to widespread poverty, famine, and social unrest among the Indonesian population.

In the early 19th century, the Dutch colonial government faced a series of challenges, including the Napoleonic Wars in Europe, which led to a temporary British occupation of Indonesia (1811-1816) under **Sir Stamford Raffles**. Following the British interregnum, the Dutch regained control of the archipelago and began a process of administrative and political reforms. The VOC was dissolved, and the Dutch government assumed direct control over its former territories, establishing the Dutch East Indies as a formal colony.

Throughout the 19th and early 20th centuries, the Dutch continued to expand and consolidate their rule over the Indonesian archipelago, facing sporadic resistance from local rulers and nationalist movements. The Dutch introduced modern infrastructure, education, and legal systems, which contributed to the development of an emerging Indonesian national consciousness.

During World War II, the Dutch East Indies fell to the Japanese Empire, which occupied the archipelago from 1942 to 1945. The Japanese occupation had a profound impact on Indonesian society, fostering a sense of nationalism and resentment towards colonial rule. Following the Japanese surrender in 1945, Indonesian nationalists, led by **Sukarno** and **Mohammad Hatta**, declared the independence of the Republic of Indonesia, sparking a violent struggle for independence against the Dutch colonial forces.

In conclusion, European colonization of Indonesia, which spanned from the early 16th to the mid-20th century, profoundly influenced the political, economic, and social landscape of the archipelago. The Dutch, in particular, left a lasting legacy on the Indonesian society, as their centuries-long rule significantly shaped the nation's identity, infrastructure, and struggle for independence. The end of European colonization in Indonesia marked the beginning of a new chapter in the country's history, as it transitioned from a collection of disparate territories to a unified nation-state.

The struggle for Indonesian independence was marked by a series of diplomatic negotiations, armed conflicts, and political turmoil. Despite the Dutch government's initial reluctance to recognize Indonesian sovereignty, mounting international pressure, particularly from the newly-formed United Nations, eventually led the Dutch to formally transfer sovereignty to the Republic of Indonesia on December 27, 1949.

The post-colonial period in Indonesia was marked by efforts to build a unified nation and address the economic, social, and political challenges inherited from centuries of colonial rule. Under the leadership of President Sukarno, the newly-independent Indonesia embarked on a program of nation-building, economic development, and social reform. However, the country also faced numerous internal and external challenges, including regional separatist movements, political instability, and the lingering influence of foreign powers.

The legacy of European colonization in Indonesia remains evident in various aspects of the nation's cultural, political, and economic life. The Dutch language, for example, continued to be used in some official and legal contexts until the mid-20th century, and many Indonesian words are of Dutch origin. Furthermore, the Dutch legal system, educational institutions, and infrastructure projects have left a lasting impact on the country.

However, the European colonization of Indonesia also left deep scars on the nation's psyche, particularly in terms of its social and economic inequalities. The exploitative colonial policies implemented by the Dutch led to widespread poverty, environmental degradation, and social unrest, which continue to reverberate in Indonesia's contemporary society.

In the decades following independence, Indonesia has made significant strides in overcoming the challenges inherited from its colonial past. The nation has made progress in areas such as economic development, education, and political stability, yet it continues to grapple with issues related to social inequality, corruption, and environmental sustainability.

Japanese occupation and the struggle for independence (1942 – 1949)

The Japanese occupation of Indonesia and the subsequent struggle for independence from 1942 to 1949 marked a critical period in the nation's history. During this time, the Indonesian people experienced harsh occupation by the Japanese Empire, which further fuelled their desire for self-determination and ultimately led to the birth of an independent Indonesia.

In 1942, as World War II raged, the Japanese Empire launched a series of successful military campaigns in Southeast Asia, ousting the European colonial powers, including the Dutch in Indonesia. The Japanese occupation of Indonesia was characterized by a harsh and exploitative regime, which sought to harness the country's vast natural resources and labour force to support their war effort. The Indonesian people faced forced labour, food shortages, and widespread human rights abuses under Japanese rule.

Despite the brutality of the occupation, the Japanese actively promoted Indonesian nationalism and sought to undermine Dutch colonial influence. The Japanese authorities established new Indonesian political and military organizations, promoted the use of the Indonesian language, and allowed for the emergence of nationalist leaders, such as Sukarno and Mohammad Hatta.

These policies, while primarily aimed at securing Japanese control over the archipelago, inadvertently fostered a sense of national unity and strengthened the Indonesian independence movement.

As the tide of World War II turned against Japan, the weakened imperial power struggled to maintain control over Indonesia. Sensing an opportunity, Indonesian nationalists accelerated their efforts to build support for an independent Indonesia. On August 17, 1945, just days after the Japanese surrender, Sukarno and Hatta proclaimed the establishment of the Republic of Indonesia, igniting a violent struggle for independence against the returning Dutch colonial forces.

The Dutch, unwilling to relinquish their colonial holdings, launched a series of military campaigns to re-establish control over the Indonesian archipelago, known as the "Dutch Police Actions." These campaigns were marked by intense fighting, atrocities on both sides, and the displacement of hundreds of thousands of civilians. The Indonesian independence movement, although poorly armed and disorganized, managed to wage a successful guerrilla war against the superior Dutch forces, drawing on widespread popular support and a deep-seated desire for self-determination.

Simultaneously, diplomatic efforts were underway to resolve the conflict. International pressure, particularly from the newly-formed United Nations, played a crucial role in pushing the Dutch government to recognize Indonesian sovereignty. The United States, a key ally of the Dutch, also exerted pressure on the Dutch government to negotiate a peaceful settlement with the Indonesian nationalists.

In 1949, after years of bitter fighting and diplomatic wrangling, the Dutch government finally acceded to international pressure and agreed to transfer sovereignty to the Republic of Indonesia. On December 27, 1949, the Dutch formally recognized the independence of Indonesia, bringing an end to more than 300 years of colonial rule and a turbulent period of struggle for the Indonesian people.

The Sukarno era (1949 - 1967)

The Sukarno era, spanning from 1949 to 1967, was a critical period in the history of modern Indonesia. As the nation's founding father and first president, Sukarno played a pivotal role in shaping the newly-independent country's political, economic, and social landscape. His leadership, characterized by strong nationalist sentiments, internationalist ambitions, and authoritarian rule, left a lasting impact on Indonesia and its people.

Upon assuming power, Sukarno faced the daunting task of uniting the diverse and disparate regions of the Indonesian archipelago under a single national identity. He promoted the concept of "Unity in Diversity" (Bhinneka Tunggal Ika), emphasizing the importance of a shared national consciousness while recognizing the diverse cultural, linguistic, and religious backgrounds of the Indonesian people. Sukarno's vision for a unified Indonesia was enshrined in the Pancasila, a set of five guiding principles that served as the ideological foundation for the new republic.

During his tenure, Sukarno pursued an ambitious program of nation-building and economic development, focusing on the expansion of infrastructure, education, and social welfare. He launched the "Guided Economy" policy, which aimed to reduce the nation's reliance on foreign investment and promote economic self-sufficiency. However, these policies were hampered by widespread corruption, inefficiency, and mismanagement, leading to an economic crisis marked by soaring inflation, a growing budget deficit, and a decline in living standards.

In the realm of international relations, Sukarno pursued a policy of non-alignment and sought to position Indonesia as a key player in the global arena. He was a founding member of the **Non-Aligned Movement**, a coalition of developing countries that sought to maintain their independence and neutrality during the Cold War. Sukarno's internationalist aspirations were also evident in his efforts to establish diplomatic relations with a diverse range of countries, including the United States, Soviet Union, and China.

Sukarno's foreign policy was marked by assertiveness and confrontational tactics, as demonstrated by his aggressive stance towards the newly-created Federation of Malaysia, which led to the violent and diplomatically damaging **Konfrontasi** (Confrontation) campaign from 1963 to 1966. Additionally, Sukarno's increasing alignment with communist countries and his support for the **Indonesian Communist Party** (PKI) further strained Indonesia's relationships with Western nations.

Domestically, Sukarno's rule became increasingly authoritarian over time, marked by the suppression of political dissent and the centralization of power. He implemented the "**Guided Democracy**" system, which curtailed the role of political parties and concentrated power in the hands of the executive branch. This system further alienated the military, leading to growing tensions between Sukarno and the armed forces.

The Sukarno era came to a sudden and tumultuous end in 1965, when a failed coup attempt, known as the **30 September Movement**, plunged the country into a period of political turmoil and violence. In the aftermath of the coup attempt, the military, led by **General Suharto**, swiftly moved to consolidate power and launched a brutal crackdown on the PKI and its supporters, resulting in the deaths of an estimated 500,000 to one million people.

In 1967, following a period of political manoeuvring and mounting pressure from the military, Sukarno was forced to relinquish power to General Suharto, who would go on to rule Indonesia for the next three decades. Sukarno's fall from power marked the end of an era characterized by nationalist fervour, ambitious development projects, and authoritarian rule, which left an indelible mark on the young nation and set the stage for the subsequent period of political, economic, and social change in Indonesia under Suharto's New Order regime.

The Sukarno era, despite its many challenges and shortcomings, was instrumental in laying the foundation for modern Indonesia. Sukarno's vision of a unified and independent nation, encapsulated in the **Pancasila**, continues to serve as the guiding principle for the Indonesian state. Furthermore, his commitment to education, infrastructure development, and social welfare laid the groundwork for future progress in these areas.

However, the era was also marred by economic mismanagement, political repression, and a growing reliance on authoritarian measures to maintain control. The consequences of these policies were felt most acutely in the economic crisis that gripped the country in the 1960s, as well as in the widespread human rights abuses that accompanied the rise of the Suharto regime.

The Suharto era (1967 - 1998)

The Suharto era, spanning from 1967 to 1998, marked a significant period in Indonesia's history, characterized by political stability, rapid economic growth, and widespread authoritarian rule. As the second president of Indonesia, General Suharto wielded considerable power, and his policies had a profound impact on the country's political, economic, and social landscape.

Upon assuming power, Suharto sought to bring stability to a nation reeling from the tumultuous events that marked the end of Sukarno's rule. He established a new regime called the "**New Order**," which aimed to restore order and promote economic development. Under Suharto's leadership, Indonesia experienced a period of rapid economic growth, fuelled by a combination of sound macroeconomic policies, foreign investment, and the exploitation of the country's vast natural resources.

The New Order government pursued a policy of economic liberalization, dismantling the protectionist measures implemented under Sukarno and opening the Indonesian economy to global markets. This approach led to a boom in exports and attracted significant foreign investment, particularly in the manufacturing and resource extraction sectors. Consequently, Indonesia experienced impressive growth rates, averaging around 7% per annum during the 1970s and 1980s, lifting millions of people out of poverty and dramatically improving living standards.

While the Suharto era witnessed remarkable economic achievements, it was also marked by rampant corruption, cronyism, and a concentration of wealth among the political and military elite. Suharto and his family amassed vast fortunes through their control of key industries and government contracts, leading to widespread public resentment and social inequality. Additionally, the exploitation of Indonesia's natural resources led to significant environmental degradation, with long-lasting consequences for the country's ecological health.

In terms of political governance, the Suharto era was defined by its authoritarian nature. Suharto consolidated power by suppressing political dissent, curbing press freedom, and co-opting key institutions, such as the military and bureaucracy. He maintained tight control over the political system by creating the **Golkar party**, which functioned as a tool for the regime to maintain power through a facade of electoral legitimacy.

Suharto's regime also emphasized national unity and social stability, promoting a policy of religious and ethnic tolerance. However, beneath the surface, tensions simmered between different religious and ethnic groups, which would later erupt in violent conflicts following the end of the New Order regime.

The Suharto era ultimately came to an abrupt end in 1998, following a severe economic crisis that engulfed Indonesia as part of the broader Asian Financial Crisis. The economic downturn exposed the weaknesses and corruption within the Indonesian economy, leading to widespread public unrest and calls for political reform. Faced with mounting pressure from both domestic and international sources, Suharto resigned from office in May 1998, bringing an end to his 31-year rule.

The Reformasi era (1998 - present)

The Reformasi era, which began in 1998, is a significant period in Indonesia's history. This era marks the transition from an authoritarian regime to a more democratic and inclusive political system. With the fall of President Suharto's New Order regime, the nation embarked on a new journey to redefine its political landscape, improve human rights, and decentralize power. The Reformasi era has seen both successes and challenges, as the nation grapples with balancing the need for stability and the demands for change.

The Reformasi era began with the fall of President Suharto, who had ruled Indonesia with an iron fist for more than three decades. The Asian financial crisis of 1997-1998 severely impacted the Indonesian economy, leading to widespread unemployment, poverty, and social unrest. As the economy collapsed, Suharto's regime became increasingly unpopular, and public pressure for political change mounted. In May 1998, Suharto resigned, paving the way for the Reformasi era.

One of the most significant changes in the Reformasi era is the transformation of Indonesia's political system. Following the fall of Suharto, Indonesia held its first democratic elections in 1999, which resulted in Abdurrahman Wahid becoming the country's first democratically elected president. The government also implemented a series of constitutional amendments between 1999 and 2002, which established term limits for the presidency, strengthened the role of the legislature, and provided for direct presidential elections.

Another critical aspect of the Reformasi era is the decentralization of power. The central government transferred significant authority to the regions, giving them more control over their resources and decision-making. This devolution of power aimed to address the grievances of various ethnic groups and foster greater inclusivity.

The Reformasi era has also witnessed the growth of press freedom and human rights. Under Suharto's regime, the media was tightly controlled, and dissent was severely punished. With the onset of Reformasi, the press gained significant freedom, which has contributed to a more vibrant and diverse media landscape. However, challenges remain, as journalists still face threats and intimidation from various groups.

Furthermore, the government has made efforts to address human rights abuses committed during the Suharto era. Several truth and reconciliation initiatives have been launched to investigate past atrocities and provide reparations for victims. While progress has been made, many human rights issues persist, including religious intolerance, violence against minorities, and the ongoing conflict in Papua.

The Indonesian economy has shown signs of recovery since the Reformasi era began. The nation's GDP has steadily grown, and poverty rates have decreased. However, the nation still faces numerous economic challenges, such as corruption, weak infrastructure, and income inequality. Addressing these issues will be crucial for the long-term sustainability of Indonesia's economic growth.

Religion, Values, and Social Norms

Indonesia, the world's largest archipelago, is home to an incredibly diverse array of religious beliefs and practices. The country's rich tapestry of faiths is a product of its unique historical and cultural evolution. Spanning over 17,000 islands, Indonesia is home to more than 270 million people, making it the fourth most populous country in the world. With a complex and dynamic religious landscape, Indonesia is a fascinating case study in religious coexistence and interfaith dialogue.

The Indonesian Constitution guarantees freedom of religion and recognizes six major religious traditions: Islam, Protestantism, Catholicism, Hinduism, Buddhism, and Confucianism. While the constitution ensures religious freedom, it also mandates that citizens adhere to one of these six officially recognized faiths. This regulation has been a subject of debate over the years, as it excludes certain minority religious groups and indigenous beliefs.

Religion

Islam is the dominant religion in Indonesia, with approximately 87% of the population identifying as Muslim. The majority of Indonesian Muslims practice **Sunni Islam**, while a smaller percentage adheres to **Shia** and other branches. Indonesian Islam is known for its moderate and diverse nature, shaped by the country's unique cultural, historical, and geographical contexts. The peaceful coexistence of different Islamic schools of thought and the influence of indigenous beliefs have resulted in a distinct and tolerant form of Islam.

Christianity is the second-largest religion in Indonesia, with around 10% of the population identifying as either Protestant (7%) or Catholic (3%). Christianity was introduced to Indonesia by European missionaries and traders during the colonial era. Today, Christians are spread throughout the archipelago, with significant concentrations in certain regions such as North Sumatra, Papua, and East Nusa Tenggara.

Hinduism, practiced by around 1.7% of the population, is primarily concentrated in the island of Bali. **Balinese Hinduism** is a unique form of the religion, with a blend of animistic, Buddhist, and Hindu elements. It is characterized by intricate rituals, a rich pantheon of gods and spirits, and a strong emphasis on artistic expression.

Buddhism and Confucianism, practiced by smaller segments of the population, have also shaped Indonesia's religious landscape. Buddhism arrived in Indonesia in the early centuries CE through trade and cultural exchange with India. While its influence has waned over time, there is still a small but vibrant Buddhist community in the country, particularly among the Chinese-Indonesian population. Confucianism, another Chinese-originated belief system, is practiced by a minority of Indonesians, primarily those of Chinese descent.

Indonesia's traditional indigenous beliefs, known as **Aliran Kepercayaan**, predate the arrival of foreign religions and continue to be practiced by some communities. These beliefs vary widely from one region to another, but they generally revolve around the worship of ancestral spirits, nature, and supernatural forces. Although not officially recognized by the government, Aliran Kepercayaan has played a crucial role in shaping Indonesia's religious and cultural identity.

Despite the diversity of faiths, Indonesia has a long history of religious tolerance and peaceful coexistence. However, this harmony has occasionally been disrupted by sectarian tensions, religious extremism, and political manipulation of religious sentiments. The government and civil society organizations have worked together to promote dialogue and understanding among different religious communities, ensuring that Indonesia remains a shining example of religious pluralism.

Social Values

At the heart of Indonesian social values lies the concept of **gotong royong**, which roughly translates to "mutual assistance" or "cooperation." This cultural norm emphasizes the importance of communal support and collaboration, encouraging individuals to work together to achieve common goals and overcome challenges. Gotong royong manifests itself in various aspects of Indonesian life, from agricultural labour-sharing practices to community-driven infrastructure projects and disaster relief efforts. This communal spirit is seen as a vital component of social harmony and unity in a diverse and geographically fragmented country.

Another prominent aspect of Indonesian social values is the emphasis on respect and deference to authority and elders. Hierarchical relationships are deeply ingrained in Indonesian society, with younger individuals expected to show respect to their elders and superiors through gestures, speech, and behaviour. This respect extends to family, religious leaders, teachers, and government officials. The value placed on respecting authority and hierarchy is rooted in historical and cultural contexts, as well as religious influences, particularly from Islam, Hinduism, and Confucianism.

Family is central to Indonesian society, with strong emphasis placed on the importance of maintaining close-knit family relationships and fulfilling familial obligations. Extended families often live in close proximity or even under the same roof, with multiple generations supporting and relying on one another. Children are expected to care for their parents as they age, while parents are responsible for providing emotional and financial support to their children. This interdependence fosters a sense of responsibility, loyalty, and love among family members.

Indonesians also place a high value on harmony and balance in social interactions. This is reflected in the concept of "rukun," which stresses the importance of maintaining peaceful relationships and avoiding conflicts. Politeness and courtesy are considered essential in interactions with others, even in the face of disagreements or disputes. The desire to maintain harmony often leads to indirect communication styles, where the intention is to avoid confrontation or causing offense.

Education is another core value in Indonesian society, seen as the key to personal development, social mobility, and national progress. Parents invest heavily in their children's education, often sacrificing their own needs to ensure their children receive the best possible schooling. The government also recognizes the importance of education, with the constitution guaranteeing access to education for all citizens.

Despite the numerous social values that unite Indonesians, the country's incredible diversity means that different ethnic groups and regions often have their own unique customs and traditions. This cultural diversity is both a source of pride and a challenge, as Indonesia strives to maintain social cohesion and harmony in the face of such diversity.

Another significant social norm in Indonesia is the emphasis on modesty and decorum in dress and behaviour. While norms surrounding modesty can vary across different regions and ethnic groups, it is generally expected that both men and women will dress modestly, particularly in public settings and religious contexts. This is especially true in predominantly Muslim areas, where women often wear headscarves and loose-fitting clothing, and men are expected to dress conservatively as well. Additionally, public displays of affection are generally frowned upon, as they are considered impolite and inappropriate.

In Indonesian society, hospitality is highly valued, and guests are often treated with great warmth and generosity. It is common for hosts to offer refreshments and food to visitors, even if the visit is unexpected or brief. Declining such offers can be considered impolite, so guests are encouraged to accept and express their gratitude. Furthermore, it is customary to remove one's shoes before entering an Indonesian home as a sign of respect for the host.

Punctuality is another area where social norms in Indonesia may differ from those in other countries. Indonesian culture often follows "jam karet," or "rubber time," which means that events and appointments may not begin at their scheduled time. While punctuality is appreciated in professional settings, it is essential to be flexible and patient when navigating social engagements in Indonesia.

Language: Key Phrases and Expressions

Indonesia is home to the Indonesian language (Bahasa Indonesia), which is the official language of the country. Here are some key phrases, expressions, and colloquial terms you might find useful or interesting when interacting with Indonesian speakers:

Key Phrases and Expressions:

- Selamat pagi - Good morning
- Selamat siang - Good afternoon
- Selamat sore - Good evening
- Selamat malam - Good night
- Apa kabar? - How are you?
- Terima kasih - Thank you
- Sama-sama - You're welcome
- Maaf - Sorry / Excuse me
- Permisi - Excuse me (to get attention or pass by)
- Ya - Yes
- Tidak - No
- Tolong - Please (used to request help)
- Berapa harganya? - How much is it?
- Di mana ...? - Where is ...?
- Nama saya ... - My name is ...
- Saya tidak mengerti - I don't understand

Colloquial expressions:

- Mas / Mbak - Informal terms to address young men (Mas) and young women (Mbak) respectively
- Boleh minta ...? - Can I have/get ...? (Informal)
- Saya mau pesan ... - I'd like to order ...

- Enak - Delicious / Tasty
- Ngomong-ngomong - By the way
- Ayo - Come on / Let's go
- Saya lagi sibuk - I'm busy right now
- Capek deh - I'm tired (Informal)
- Mau kemana? - Where are you going? (Informal)
- Nggak apa-apa - It's okay / No problem (Informal)

Keep in mind that Indonesian is a very diverse country with many regional languages, so you may encounter different slang or expressions depending on where you are. However, these basic phrases and expressions should be understandable to most Indonesian speakers.

Famous Indonesians

- R.A. Kartini: A heroine and women's rights advocate during the late 19th and early 20th centuries.
- Cut Nyak Dhien: A national heroine who fought against Dutch colonial rule during the Aceh War.
- Diponegoro: A Javanese prince who led the Java War against the Dutch colonial forces.
- Gajah Mada: A military leader and prime minister of the Majapahit Empire during the 14th century.
- Hang Tuah: A legendary Malay warrior who served the Sultan of Malacca during the 15th century.
- Pattimura: Ambonese soldier who led a rebellion against Dutch colonial forces in Maluku Islands.
- Raden Saleh: 19th-century Indonesian artist, considered pioneer of modern Indonesian painting.
- Pangeran Antasari: Banjarese prince who led a war against Dutch colonial forces in Borneo.

Famous Indonesian Legends & Myths

- Malin Kundang: A man who turns into stone as punishment for disrespecting his mother after gaining wealth.
- Roro Jonggrang: A princess who tricks a prince into constructing a thousand temples overnight to avoid marrying him, leading to the creation of the Prambanan temple complex.
- Keong Mas: A tale of a princess cursed to live as a golden snail, eventually restored to her human form by a fisherman's kind actions.
- Barong: The mythical creature representing good in Balinese culture, locked in an eternal battle against the evil witch Rangda.

- <u>Nyi Roro Kidul</u>: A mythical Javanese queen ruling the Southern Ocean, believed to protect and bring prosperity to the Mataram kingdom.
- <u>Bawang Merah Bawang Putih</u>: A Cinderella-like tale about two stepsisters, one kind and the other cruel, ultimately receiving their respective rewards and punishments.
- <u>Sangkuriang</u>: A tragic love story between a man and his long-lost mother, culminating in the creation of the Tangkuban Perahu volcano.

4. ADAPTING TO DAILY LIFE IN INDONESIA

Housing and Accommodations

Settling into daily life in Indonesia may initially seem daunting due to the cultural, linguistic, and geographical differences. However, with some research, planning, and an open mind, you can adapt to life in this diverse and vibrant country. One of the essential aspects of adapting to life in Indonesia is finding suitable housing and accommodations. This guide will provide you with an overview of the various housing options available and tips for finding the right place to live.

Types of Accommodations

In Indonesia, there is a wide range of housing options, from traditional Indonesian homes to modern apartments and expatriate compounds. The type of accommodation that is best suited for you will depend on your budget, lifestyle preferences, and location.

Traditional Indonesian Houses: These are typically single-story structures made of wood, bamboo, or brick, with a sloping roof and a small yard. While these homes may lack modern amenities, they offer an authentic living experience and are often more affordable than other options.

Apartments and Condominiums: In larger cities like Jakarta, Bandung, or Surabaya, you can find numerous apartment complexes and condominiums catering to various budgets and preferences. These units often come with modern facilities such as air conditioning, security, and recreational amenities like swimming pools and gyms.

Expatriate Compounds: In some areas, particularly in Jakarta and Bali, there are residential compounds specifically designed for expatriates. These gated communities often offer fully furnished homes or apartments, with security, shared facilities, and a sense of community among expat residents.

Kos (boarding houses) or Rumah Kost: These are affordable, rented rooms within a larger house, typically aimed at students or budget-conscious individuals. They usually include basic amenities and shared facilities such as a kitchen and bathroom.

Choosing a Location

When looking for housing in Indonesia, consider factors such as proximity to your workplace, access to public transportation, local amenities (schools, hospitals, shopping centers), and the overall atmosphere of the neighbourhood. Research various neighbourhoods and consult with locals or expatriates who have experience living in the area.

Rental Process

Renting a property in Indonesia can be a straightforward process, but it's essential to understand local customs and practices. Some tips for a smooth rental experience include:

Engage a Real Estate Agent: A reliable agent can help you navigate the local property market, find suitable accommodations, and negotiate the lease terms.

Understand the Lease Terms: Rental contracts in Indonesia may be different from what you're used to in your home country. Ensure you understand the lease duration, payment terms, and any additional charges or fees.

Be Prepared to Negotiate: It is common to negotiate rental prices and lease terms in Indonesia. Don't be afraid to discuss these with the landlord or agent.

Inspect the Property: Before signing the lease, thoroughly inspect the property and make note of any issues or necessary repairs. Ensure these are addressed before moving in.

Settling In

Once you have found suitable housing, take some time to familiarize yourself with your new surroundings. Get to know your neighbours, explore local markets and shops, and learn about the customs and etiquette of your new community.

Transportation and Getting Around

Navigating the vast Indonesian archipelago and its bustling cities can be challenging, particularly for newcomers. However, familiarizing yourself with the various modes of transportation and understanding local travel customs can make getting around Indonesia much easier. This guide will provide an overview of transportation options and tips for navigating daily life in Indonesia.

Public Transportation

Indonesia's public transportation system varies by region, and larger cities tend to have more extensive networks. Some of the common public transportation options include:

Buses: City buses are available in most major cities, providing an affordable way to get around. However, they can be crowded, and routes may be confusing for newcomers.

TransJakarta Bus Rapid Transit (BRT): In Jakarta, the BRT system offers a more organized and comfortable public transportation experience. Dedicated lanes and air-conditioned buses make this a popular choice for commuters.

Commuter Trains: In cities like Jakarta, Bogor, Depok, Tangerang, and Bekasi, commuter trains provide a reliable and cost-effective way to travel between urban and suburban areas. However, they can be crowded during peak hours.

Angkot/Mikrolet: These are small, privately-owned minibuses or vans that operate on set routes. They are an affordable and flexible option, although they can be crowded and may not always follow a strict schedule.

Taxis and Ride-Hailing Services

Taxis are widely available in most Indonesian cities and can be hailed on the street or booked through a taxi company. It's advisable to use a reputable taxi company, as not all taxis use meters. Ride-hailing services like **Grab** and **Gojek** have become increasingly popular and offer a convenient alternative to traditional taxis. These services also provide motorcycle taxis (**ojek**) for a faster and more affordable option, particularly in areas with heavy traffic.

Private Vehicles

Many expats and locals opt to use private vehicles for their daily transportation needs. Cars and motorcycles are the most common choices, but be prepared to navigate heavy traffic, especially in larger cities. Before driving in Indonesia, ensure you have a valid driver's license and understand local traffic rules and customs.

Bicycles and Pedestrian Travel

In some areas, particularly in smaller towns or residential neighbourhoods, bicycles can be a viable transportation option. However, the lack of dedicated cycling lanes and heavy traffic in urban areas can make cycling challenging. Walking is possible for short distances, but be aware that pedestrian infrastructure may be lacking, and it's essential to remain vigilant when crossing streets.

Long-Distance Travel

For travel between cities and islands, Indonesia offers various transportation options, including:

Air Travel: With numerous domestic airports, flying is often the fastest and most convenient way to travel long distances within Indonesia.

Trains: Train travel is available on Java and Sumatra, offering a comfortable and scenic way to explore these islands.

Buses: Long-distance buses connect many cities and towns across the country, but the quality and comfort of these buses can vary.

Ferries: Indonesia's extensive ferry network connects many of its islands, providing an affordable and leisurely way to explore the archipelago.

Education and Schooling Options

When moving to Indonesia, particularly for those with children, understanding the available education and schooling options is crucial. The Indonesian education system offers various options, including public schools, private schools, and international schools, each with its own advantages and challenges. This guide will provide an overview of the different education options and help you make informed decisions about your family's schooling needs in Indonesia.

Public Schools

Public schools in Indonesia are government-funded and follow the national curriculum. Education is compulsory for children aged 7 to 15 years and is divided into primary (6 years), junior secondary (3 years), and senior secondary (3 years) levels. While public schools are accessible and affordable, they often face challenges such as overcrowded classrooms, limited resources, and varying levels of teaching quality. Additionally, language barriers may pose a challenge, as the primary language of instruction is Bahasa Indonesia.

Private Schools

Private schools in Indonesia are independently funded and typically offer smaller class sizes and more resources compared to public schools. Some private schools follow the national curriculum, while others adopt alternative curricula, such as the Montessori or Waldorf approach. Private schools often provide a more personalized learning experience and may offer additional extracurricular activities. However, tuition fees can vary significantly, and some private schools may still use Bahasa Indonesia as the primary language of instruction.

International Schools

International schools are a popular choice for expatriates and affluent Indonesian families seeking a global education for their children. These schools typically follow internationally recognized curricula, such as the International Baccalaureate (IB), the British National Curriculum, or the American curriculum. International schools often boast excellent facilities, highly qualified teachers, and a diverse student body. The primary language of instruction is usually English, making it easier for expatriate children to adapt.

However, international schools can be quite expensive, with tuition fees often significantly higher than private schools. Additionally, international schools are predominantly located in major cities such as Jakarta, Bali, and Surabaya, which may limit options for those living in other areas.

Home-schooling

Home-schooling is another option for families in Indonesia, particularly for those who prefer a more personalized and flexible approach to education. Home-schooling allows parents to choose their children's curriculum and learning pace, and it can be an excellent option for families who frequently move or live in remote locations. However, home-schooling requires a significant time investment from parents and may limit children's opportunities for socialization.

Choosing the Right School

When selecting a school for your children in Indonesia, consider factors such as:

Curriculum: Ensure the chosen curriculum aligns with your family's educational goals and allows for a smooth transition if you plan to move to another country in the future.

Accreditation: Look for schools with recognized accreditations to ensure a high standard of education.

Location: Consider the proximity of the school to your home and workplace to minimize travel time.

Language of Instruction: For expatriate families, ensuring that the language of instruction is compatible with your child's language skills is crucial.

Extracurricular Activities: Schools that offer a range of extracurricular activities can provide a more well-rounded education and opportunities for socialization.

Budget: Be mindful of tuition fees and any additional costs associated with schooling, such as uniforms, books, and transportation.

Healthcare and Medical Facilities

Access to quality healthcare is an essential consideration when moving to a new country. In Indonesia, the healthcare system is a mix of public and private facilities, offering various levels of care and quality. This guide will provide an overview of the healthcare system in Indonesia, as well as tips for navigating medical facilities and ensuring you have access to the care you need.

Public Healthcare

Indonesia's public healthcare system is funded by the government and provides basic medical services to citizens and residents. The country has made significant strides in improving access to healthcare in recent years, with the introduction of the national health insurance program (**BPJS Kesehatan**) in 2014. This program aims to provide universal health coverage for all Indonesian citizens and covers a range of services, including primary care, hospitalization, and emergency care.

While public healthcare is accessible and affordable, public hospitals and clinics may face challenges such as overcrowding, limited resources, and varying levels of care quality. Additionally, language barriers can pose a challenge for expatriates, as most healthcare professionals in public facilities primarily speak Bahasa Indonesia.

Private Healthcare

For those seeking a higher standard of care, private healthcare facilities are available in major cities like Jakarta, Surabaya, and Bali. Private hospitals and clinics generally offer more modern facilities, better-equipped resources, and shorter waiting times compared to public healthcare providers. Many private healthcare professionals also speak English, making communication easier for expatriates.

However, private healthcare can be considerably more expensive than public healthcare, and not all services may be covered by insurance. It's essential to research private healthcare options and ensure you have adequate insurance coverage to cover any potential medical expenses.

International Hospitals and Clinics

In larger cities, international hospitals and clinics cater specifically to the needs of expatriates and foreign visitors. These facilities often have internationally trained staff, offer a higher standard of care, and are more likely to have English-speaking healthcare professionals. International hospitals and clinics typically provide a range of services, from primary care and specialist consultations to emergency care and dental services.

While these facilities offer a more familiar healthcare experience for expatriates, they can be significantly more expensive than both public and private healthcare providers in Indonesia. As with private healthcare, it's crucial to have comprehensive insurance coverage to manage the costs associated with international healthcare facilities.

Health Insurance

Expatriates living in Indonesia should ensure they have comprehensive health insurance to cover any potential medical expenses. This may involve securing an international health insurance plan or obtaining coverage through an employer-sponsored plan. Ensure your insurance plan covers a range of services, from primary care and specialist consultations to hospitalization and emergency care.

Precautions and Preparedness

To maintain good health while living in Indonesia, it's important to take necessary precautions and be prepared for any potential health issues. Some tips for staying healthy in Indonesia include:

- Stay up-to-date with vaccinations and follow any recommended vaccination schedules for your destination.
- Practice good hygiene, such as regular handwashing, to reduce the risk of illness.
- Drink bottled or boiled water, as tap water may not be safe for consumption.
- Be mindful of food safety and avoid consuming undercooked or unhygienic food.
- Use insect repellent and take other precautions to avoid mosquito-borne diseases, such as dengue fever and malaria.

- Keep a well-stocked first aid kit and a list of emergency contacts, including local healthcare providers and your insurance company.

Safety and Security

When moving to a new country, it's essential to familiarize yourself with local safety and security considerations. While Indonesia is generally considered a safe destination for expatriates and tourists, it's important to be aware of potential risks and take appropriate precautions to ensure a secure and enjoyable experience. This guide will provide an overview of safety and security concerns in Indonesia and offer tips for staying safe.

Petty Crime

As in many countries, petty crime, such as pickpocketing and bag-snatching, can be a concern in crowded areas, public transportation, and tourist hotspots. To minimize the risk of petty crime:

- Be aware of your surroundings and stay vigilant in crowded places.
- Keep your belongings secure and avoid displaying valuable items, such as expensive jewellery or electronics.
- Use a money belt or hidden pouch to store important documents and money.
- Avoid walking alone in unfamiliar or poorly lit areas, especially at night.

Scams and Fraud

Scams and fraud targeting tourists and expatriates can occur in Indonesia. Common scams include fake tour operators, currency exchange scams, and taxi scams. To protect yourself from scams:

- Be cautious when approached by strangers offering unsolicited assistance or deals.
- Research and book tours or activities through reputable companies.
- Use official currency exchange services and count your money carefully before leaving the counter.
- Use reputable taxi companies or ride-hailing apps like Grab or Gojek.

Traffic Safety

Traffic in Indonesia, particularly in larger cities like Jakarta, can be chaotic and pose a significant safety risk. Accidents and road fatalities are not uncommon, and road conditions can be poor in some areas. To stay safe on Indonesian roads:

- Use seatbelts whenever available and ensure children use appropriate car seats.

- Avoid driving a car or motorcycle unless you are familiar with local traffic rules and customs.
- Use reputable taxi services or ride-hailing apps for transportation.
- Exercise caution when crossing streets, as pedestrian infrastructure may be lacking, and drivers may not always yield to pedestrians.

Natural Disasters

Indonesia is prone to natural disasters, such as earthquakes, volcanic eruptions, and tsunamis. Familiarize yourself with the potential risks in your area and be prepared for emergencies by:

- Staying informed about local news and weather updates.
- Having an emergency preparedness plan, including a well-stocked emergency kit and a list of emergency contacts.
- Following local authorities' advice and evacuation orders in the event of a natural disaster.

Personal Security

While violent crime is relatively rare in Indonesia, it's important to be aware of personal security risks and take appropriate precautions. To maintain personal security:

- Register with your country's embassy or consulate upon arrival in Indonesia.
- Avoid engaging in high-risk activities or behaviours, such as drug use or excessive alcohol consumption.
- Be cautious when sharing personal information with strangers or on social media.
- Ensure your accommodation is secure and consider using additional safety measures, such as a doorstop or personal alarm.

5. NAVIGATING SOCIAL INTERACTIONS AI ETIQUETTE

Making Friends and Building Connections

Navigating social interactions and etiquette is an important aspect of adapting to daily life in another country. Building connections and making friends with locals and other expatriates can greatly enhance your experience and help you acclimate to the culture more quickly. Here are some tips for making friends and building connections while respecting local social etiquette:

Language

Learning some basic phrases can go a long way in making friends and breaking down communication barriers. Even if your language skills are limited, locals will appreciate your effort to speak their language. Additionally, consider enrolling in a language class, which can also serve as an opportunity to meet new people and practice your language skills.

Cultural understanding

Familiarize yourself with local customs, traditions, and social norms to better understand and navigate social interactions. Being aware of and respecting local etiquette, such as greetings, table manners, and gift-giving customs, will help you make a positive impression and build rapport with locals.

Networking events and social clubs

Attend networking events, expatriate meetups, and social clubs to meet like-minded individuals and expand your social circle. There are numerous groups and organizations catering to expatriates, offering opportunities for cultural exchange, language practice, and shared interests.

Hobbies and interests

Pursue your hobbies and interests by joining clubs, teams, or classes. Participating in activities that you enjoy will provide a natural setting to connect with others who share your interests, making it easier to build friendships.

Social media and messaging apps

Social media platforms and messaging apps are usually widely used and can be an excellent tool for staying connected and organizing social events. Be sure to exchange contact information with new acquaintances and join relevant groups to stay informed about upcoming events and activities.

Be open and approachable

When interacting with locals and other expatriates, be open, approachable, and willing to engage in conversation. Share your experiences, ask questions, and show genuine interest in learning about culture and the experiences of others. Demonstrating curiosity and an open-minded attitude will make you more approachable and help you build connections more easily.

Patience and persistence

Building meaningful friendships takes time and effort, especially when navigating cultural differences. Be patient and persistent in your efforts to connect with others, and remember that building strong relationships may require additional time and understanding.

Social Customs and Taboos

Indonesia is a diverse and multicultural country, with over 300 ethnic groups and a variety of religious beliefs. As a result, the social customs and taboos can vary significantly across the archipelago. However, there are some general guidelines that can help you navigate Indonesian society and avoid offending local sensibilities. Here are some key social customs and taboos to keep in mind when living in or visiting Indonesia:

Respect for Elders and Authority Figures

Indonesians highly value respect for elders and authority figures. It's essential to address them with appropriate titles (e.g., Pak for men, Ibu for women) and to always show deference in conversations or when receiving advice.

Harmony and Politeness

Indonesians generally prioritize maintaining harmony and avoiding conflict in social interactions. Politeness and indirect communication are valued, and it's important to avoid confrontational behaviour or blunt criticism. Instead, try to express your thoughts diplomatically and be sensitive to non-verbal cues in conversations.

Dress Conservatively

Dressing modestly is essential, particularly in rural areas and religious communities. While Western-style clothing is common in urban areas, it's still essential to dress appropriately, avoiding revealing or provocative attire. When visiting religious sites, such as mosques or temples, ensure you cover your shoulders, legs, and, if necessary, your head.

Right Hand Etiquette

The left hand is considered impure in Indonesian culture, so always use your right hand when eating, giving or receiving items, and shaking hands. If you need to use your left hand, it's polite to apologize or acknowledge the gesture.

Shoes Off Indoors

When entering someone's home or a place of worship, it's customary to remove your shoes. This practice shows respect for the host and the space and helps maintain cleanliness.

Public Displays of Affection

Public displays of affection (PDA) are generally frowned upon in Indonesia, especially in more conservative areas. It's best to avoid excessive touching, hugging, or kissing in public to respect local sensitivities.

Religious Observances

Indonesia is a predominantly Muslim country, but other religions such as Christianity, Hinduism, and Buddhism are also practiced. Be respectful of religious practices and rituals, and accommodate prayer times or fasting periods when interacting with people of different faiths.

Photography

Always ask for permission before taking photographs of people or their property. In some areas, taking photos of government buildings or military installations may be prohibited. Be aware of local restrictions and always respect people's privacy.

Alcohol Consumption

While alcohol is available in many parts of Indonesia, consumption should be done discreetly, especially in predominantly Muslim areas. In some regions, like Aceh, alcohol is entirely banned. It's essential to be respectful of local customs and avoid public intoxication.

Gifts and Souvenirs

When invited to someone's home, it's customary to bring a small gift, such as sweets or fruits. If you receive a gift, it's polite to reciprocate with a gift of equal or lesser value.

Dining and Food Culture

Indonesian cuisine is as diverse as its people, drawing from various regional and cultural influences throughout the archipelago. From the spicy flavours of Sumatra to the rich and aromatic dishes of Java, Indonesian food culture offers a unique and vibrant experience for the adventurous palate. Here are some key aspects of Indonesian dining and food culture that you should know:

Staple Ingredients

Rice is the primary staple in Indonesia, served with most meals and playing a central role in the country's food culture. Other staples include corn, cassava, and various types of noodles. Protein sources include chicken, beef, and fish, while tofu and tempeh are popular vegetarian options. Coconut milk, chili peppers, and an array of spices, such as coriander, turmeric, and galangal, are frequently used to create rich, flavourful dishes.

Traditional Dishes

Indonesia boasts a wide variety of traditional dishes, with each region having its specialties. Some popular Indonesian dishes include:

- Nasi Goreng: Indonesian fried rice, often served with a fried egg, chicken or shrimp, and vegetables.
- Satay: Grilled skewers of marinated meat, usually served with peanut sauce.
- Rendang: A slow-cooked, spicy beef dish originating from West Sumatra.
- Gado-Gado: A vegetable salad served with peanut sauce dressing and boiled eggs.
- Soto: A traditional Indonesian soup made with various ingredients, such as chicken, beef, or vegetables, and flavoured with aromatic spices.

Dining Etiquette

When dining in Indonesia, it's essential to be aware of local customs and etiquette:

- Use your right hand for eating, as the left hand is considered impure.
- Wait for the host to invite you to start eating before beginning your meal.
- It's common to eat with your hands, particularly when enjoying traditional Indonesian dishes. However, utensils are usually provided in restaurants or when eating Western-style meals.
- When dining in someone's home, it's customary to bring a small gift, such as fruits or sweets.

Street Food and Warungs

Street food is a crucial part of Indonesian food culture, with an array of delicious and affordable options available throughout the country. Food stalls or carts, known as "kaki lima," offer a variety of dishes, from savoury snacks to complete meals. Warungs are small, family-owned eateries that serve home-style Indonesian cuisine at affordable prices. These establishments provide an authentic taste of Indonesian food and are an excellent way to explore local flavours.

Eating Out

Indonesian cities and tourist destinations offer a range of dining options, from local warungs and street food vendors to upscale restaurants serving international cuisine. While traditional Indonesian dishes are widely available, you'll also find various international foods, particularly in larger cities like Jakarta and Bali.

Drinking Culture

Although Indonesia is a predominantly Muslim country, alcoholic beverages are available in most urban areas and tourist destinations. However, alcohol consumption should be done discreetly, particularly in more conservative regions. Non-alcoholic beverages, such as fruit juices, tea, and coffee, are widely consumed and readily available.

6. BUSINESS ETIQUETTE AND PRACTICES

Building Trust and Relationships

In Indonesian business culture, building trust and establishing strong relationships are crucial for successful collaboration and negotiation. Understanding and adhering to local business etiquette and practices can significantly enhance your professional interactions in Indonesia. Here are some essential tips for building trust and relationships in the Indonesian business environment:

Respect Hierarchy and Seniority

Indonesian business culture is hierarchical, with age, experience, and position playing significant roles in decision-making processes. It's important to show respect to those in higher positions, as well as elders. Use appropriate titles when addressing colleagues and business partners, such as "Pak" for men and "Ibu" for women, followed by their first name.

Polite and Indirect Communication

Indonesians generally prioritize maintaining harmony and avoiding confrontation in their interactions. Diplomacy and indirect communication are highly valued. Be mindful of your tone and body language, and avoid being overly critical or confrontational in discussions. It's essential to read between the lines and pay attention to non-verbal cues that may indicate disagreement or discomfort.

Personal Relationships and Networking

Building personal relationships is vital for successful business dealings in Indonesia. It's not uncommon for initial meetings to focus on getting to know one another rather than discussing business matters. Be prepared to engage in small talk and share information about your family, hobbies, and interests. Attending social events and networking opportunities can also help strengthen your connections with Indonesian business partners.

Patience and Flexibility

Time is often perceived more fluidly in Indonesia, and punctuality may not be strictly observed. Be patient and flexible when dealing with delays or last-minute changes in appointments. It's also essential to remain open-minded and adaptable when navigating the Indonesian business environment.

Gift-Giving

In Indonesian business culture, exchanging gifts can be an essential part of relationship-building. Bring a small token of appreciation, such as a souvenir from your home country, to present to your Indonesian counterparts during your first meeting. Ensure that your gift is wrapped and presented with both hands. Remember to use your right hand or both hands, as the left hand is considered impure.

Business Attire

While the climate in Indonesia is warm and humid, formal business attire is still expected in most professional settings. Men should wear a suit and tie, while women should opt for conservative dresses, skirts, or pantsuits. Avoid wearing revealing or provocative clothing, as modesty is valued in Indonesian culture.

Religious Sensitivities

Be aware of and respectful towards the religious practices and observances of your Indonesian colleagues. During the holy month of Ramadan, for example, be mindful that many Indonesians will be fasting during daylight hours, which may affect working hours and business practices.

Language

Although English is widely spoken in Indonesian business circles, learning a few basic phrases in Bahasa Indonesia can be an excellent way to demonstrate your interest in and respect for local culture. Speaking the local language can help foster stronger connections with your Indonesian business partners.

Dress Code and Appearance

Dress code and appearance play an essential role in making a good impression and showing respect for local customs when conducting business in Indonesia. Understanding and adhering to the appropriate dress code is crucial for successful professional interactions in the Indonesian business environment. Here are some guidelines on dress code and appearance for business engagements in Indonesia:

Formal Business Attire

In most professional settings, formal business attire is expected. Men should wear a suit and tie, while women should opt for conservative dresses, skirts, or pantsuits. In some less formal situations or during hot weather, it may be acceptable for men to wear a dress shirt without a tie, but it's best to follow the lead of your Indonesian counterparts.

Modesty and Conservatism

Modesty is highly valued in Indonesian culture, particularly in more conservative areas or among religious communities. Women should ensure their clothing covers the shoulders, cleavage, and knees. Avoid wearing tight or revealing clothing, as this may be considered inappropriate. Men should also dress conservatively and avoid wearing shorts or sleeveless shirts in professional settings.

Colour Choices

When selecting your business attire, opt for neutral or muted colours, such as black, navy, grey, or beige. These colours convey a sense of professionalism and respect for local customs. Bright or flashy colours may be perceived as ostentatious and should generally be avoided.

Footwear

Closed-toe, polished shoes are the most appropriate choice for both men and women in professional settings. Sandals or flip-flops are generally considered too casual for business engagements. When entering someone's home or a place of worship, it's customary to remove your shoes, so it's a good idea to wear footwear that can be easily taken off and put back on.

Grooming and Personal Hygiene

Personal grooming and hygiene are essential aspects of the Indonesian business dress code. Ensure your hair is neat and clean, and men should be clean-shaven or have well-groomed facial hair. Keep makeup and perfume or cologne subtle, as strong scents may be considered offensive. Given the warm and humid climate, it's also essential to maintain good personal hygiene and use deodorant.

Accessories and Jewellery

Accessories and jewellery should be kept minimal and understated to convey professionalism and respect for local customs. Men should avoid wearing excessive jewellery, such as large rings or bracelets, while women should opt for simple and elegant pieces.

Business Cards and Introductions

Exchanging business cards and making introductions are essential aspects of Indonesian business culture. Proper etiquette during these interactions can help create a positive impression and lay the foundation for successful business relationships. Here are some guidelines for exchanging business cards and making introductions in Indonesia:

Business Cards

Business cards are an important tool for making connections and establishing professional relationships in Indonesia. Always carry a sufficient supply of cards with you when attending meetings or networking events.

- When presenting your business card, use your right hand or both hands, as the left hand is considered impure in Indonesian culture. If you are left-handed, it's polite to acknowledge the gesture and apologize for using your left hand.

- It's a good idea to have one side of your business card printed in English and the other in Bahasa Indonesia, demonstrating your respect for the local language and culture.

- When receiving a business card, take a moment to read it carefully and show interest in the person's title and company. This gesture shows respect and appreciation for the exchange.

- Avoid writing on or folding the business card in the presence of the person who gave it to you, as this may be considered disrespectful. Instead, store the card in a cardholder or a safe place in your wallet or purse.

Introductions

Introductions are a crucial aspect of establishing trust and rapport in Indonesian business culture. Here are some tips for making introductions in a professional setting:

- When introducing yourself or others, use formal titles such as "Pak" for men and "Ibu" for women, followed by their first name. This practice shows respect and acknowledges the individual's position or seniority.

- It's customary to shake hands with both men and women during introductions, using a light grip and accompanied by a slight bow or nod of the head. Use your right hand for handshakes, as the left hand is considered impure.

- In some cases, your Indonesian counterpart may place their left hand on their right forearm during the handshake as a sign of respect. This gesture is more common among older or more traditional individuals.

- Always greet the most senior person in the room first, followed by the others in descending order of seniority. This practice demonstrates respect for hierarchy, which is an essential aspect of Indonesian business culture.

- When greeting a group of people, it's customary to greet each person individually, starting with the most senior member and working your way down the hierarchy.

Communication Styles and Nonverbal Cues

Understanding and adapting to the communication styles and nonverbal cues in Indonesian business culture can significantly enhance your professional interactions. Indonesian communication tends to be indirect, diplomatic, and focused on maintaining harmony. Here are some essential aspects of communication styles and nonverbal cues in the Indonesian business environment:

Indirect Communication

Indonesians generally prioritize maintaining harmony and avoiding confrontation in their interactions. Diplomacy and indirect communication are highly valued. Be mindful of your tone and body language, and avoid being overly critical or confrontational in discussions. It's essential to read between the lines and pay attention to non-verbal cues that may indicate disagreement or discomfort.

Politeness and Formality

Politeness is a crucial aspect of communication in Indonesia. Always use formal titles such as "Pak" for men and "Ibu" for women, followed by their first name. Maintain a respectful tone and avoid using slang or colloquial language, especially in formal business settings.

Nonverbal Cues

Paying attention to nonverbal cues can provide valuable insights into your Indonesian counterparts' feelings or opinions. Some common nonverbal cues in Indonesian culture include:

Facial expressions: Indonesians may use facial expressions to convey emotions or messages. A smile can indicate happiness, agreement, or even discomfort. Pay attention to subtle changes in facial expressions during conversations.

Eye contact: In Indonesian culture, direct eye contact can be considered aggressive or impolite. It's better to maintain a soft gaze or periodically avert your eyes to show respect, especially when interacting with someone senior or of higher status.

Gestures: Use gestures sparingly, as excessive gesturing may be perceived as aggressive or disrespectful. Avoid pointing with your finger, as this is considered impolite. Instead, use your thumb or an open hand to indicate a direction or person.

Silence and Pauses

In Indonesian communication, silence and pauses are often used to convey messages or allow for reflection. Do not feel pressured to fill every moment with conversation. Embrace silence and use it as an opportunity to observe nonverbal cues and gauge the atmosphere of the discussion.

Saving Face

Saving face is essential in Indonesian culture, and it's crucial to avoid causing embarrassment or loss of face for your counterparts. Be diplomatic and tactful in your communication, and avoid criticizing or confronting others in public. If you need to address an issue or disagreement, do so privately and with sensitivity.

Holding Hands

At times a male colleague may hold your hand, this is usually when conversing. This is normally when the other person has a level of trust and wishes to have an in-depth and private conversation. It is in no way in a sexual manner as it would be in many western countries. Whatever your 'prejudices or bias' you should take it in the manner it is offered and not recoil.

7. OFFICE CULTURE AND HIERARCHIES

Respect for Authority and Seniority

In Indonesian office culture, respect for authority and seniority is deeply ingrained and plays a vital role in daily interactions and decision-making processes. Recognizing and adhering to this hierarchical structure can greatly contribute to successful professional relationships in Indonesia. Here are some important aspects of Indonesian office culture regarding respect for authority and seniority:

Hierarchy and Decision-Making

Indonesian businesses tend to have a top-down management structure, with decision-making authority centralized among senior executives or managers. Employees are expected to follow the directions of their superiors and may be hesitant to question or challenge their decisions. As a foreign professional, it's essential to respect this hierarchical structure and direct your queries or suggestions to the appropriate person within the organization.

Addressing Superiors and Colleagues

Using formal titles and addressing people by their proper names is a key aspect of showing respect for authority and seniority in Indonesian office culture. When referring to colleagues or superiors, use "Pak" for men and "Ibu" for women, followed by their first name. Avoid using first names alone, as this may be considered overly casual or disrespectful.

Deference and Humility

Deference and humility are highly valued in Indonesian office culture. Employees are expected to be modest in their accomplishments and avoid boasting or self-promotion. When offering suggestions or opinions, do so tactfully and diplomatically to avoid appearing confrontational or disrespectful to authority.

Giving and Receiving Feedback

In the interest of maintaining harmony, Indonesians may be reluctant to provide direct negative feedback or criticism, particularly in public settings. If you need to provide feedback, do so privately and constructively. Similarly, be prepared to receive feedback indirectly or through nonverbal cues. Pay attention to subtle hints or suggestions that may indicate areas for improvement or disagreement.

Respect for Age and Experience

Age and experience are highly regarded in Indonesian office culture, and employees are expected to show respect and deference to their elders or more experienced colleagues. Recognize the contributions of senior colleagues and be open to learning from their expertise and knowledge.

Decision-Making Processes

In Indonesian business culture, decision-making processes often differ from those in Western countries. Understanding these differences and adapting your approach can significantly enhance your professional interactions and collaborations in Indonesia. Here are some key aspects of decision-making processes in Indonesian business culture:

Hierarchical Structure

Indonesian businesses typically have a hierarchical organizational structure, with decision-making authority centralized among senior executives or managers. Employees are expected to follow the directions of their superiors and may be hesitant to question or challenge their decisions. As a foreign professional, it's crucial to respect this hierarchical structure and direct your queries or suggestions to the appropriate person within the organization.

Consensus-Building

Consensus-building is an essential aspect of decision-making in Indonesian business culture. Managers and executives may consult with their subordinates and colleagues to gather input and opinions before making decisions. This process can be time-consuming, as it aims to ensure that everyone's perspectives are considered, and harmony within the group is maintained. Patience and flexibility are essential during this process, as reaching a consensus may take longer than in more individualistic cultures.

Saving Face

The concept of saving face is deeply ingrained in Indonesian culture and can significantly influence the decision-making process. Indonesian businesspeople may avoid direct confrontation or disagreement, preferring instead to communicate indirectly or use diplomacy to express their opinions. Be mindful of this cultural preference and avoid being overly critical or confrontational in discussions.

Personal Relationships

Building trust and personal relationships are critical to successful decision-making in Indonesia. Businesspeople may be more inclined to make decisions based on their connections and relationships with others, rather than solely on objective criteria. Investing time and effort into establishing strong relationships with your Indonesian counterparts can have a significant impact on your ability to influence decisions and collaborate effectively.

Patience and Flexibility

Given the emphasis on consensus-building and maintaining harmony, decision-making in Indonesian business culture can be slower than in some Western countries. It's important to approach the decision-making process with patience, flexibility, and an understanding of the cultural context. Being adaptable and open-minded can help facilitate smoother negotiations and contribute to successful outcomes.

8. BUSINESS MEETINGS AND NEGOTIATIONS

Scheduling and Punctuality

Scheduling and punctuality are essential aspects of conducting business meetings and negotiations in Indonesia. By understanding the local expectations and customs related to scheduling and punctuality, you can ensure smooth and successful interactions with your Indonesian counterparts. Here are some key points to consider:

Scheduling Meetings

- When scheduling business meetings in Indonesia, it's best to arrange them well in advance, preferably a few weeks ahead of time. This allows your Indonesian counterparts to prepare and allocate the necessary time for the meeting.

- When proposing a date and time for the meeting, be mindful of local holidays, religious observances, and working hours. Indonesia is a predominantly Muslim country, and many businesses close or have reduced hours during the holy month of Ramadan.

- It's a good idea to confirm the meeting date, time, and venue a few days before the scheduled meeting to ensure everyone is on the same page.

Punctuality

- While punctuality is generally appreciated in Indonesian business culture, it's important to note that the concept of time can be more relaxed than in some Western countries. It's not uncommon for meetings to start late or for participants to arrive a few minutes after the scheduled time.

- As a foreign professional, it's important to be punctual and arrive on time for meetings, even if your Indonesian counterparts may be more flexible with their arrival time. Your punctuality demonstrates your commitment and respect for their time.

- Traffic congestion, particularly in major cities like Jakarta, can cause significant delays. Be sure to factor in extra travel time when planning your schedule and consider informing your hosts if you anticipate being late due to unavoidable circumstances.

Flexibility and Adaptability

- Be prepared for changes in the meeting schedule or agenda, as Indonesian business culture tends to be more flexible and adaptable than some Western cultures. This flexibility may include last-minute adjustments, rescheduled meetings, or changes in the meeting's focus.
- Embrace this adaptability and be open to changes as they arise, recognizing that such flexibility is a normal part of conducting business in Indonesia.

Meeting Structure and Protocol

Understanding the structure and protocol of business meetings in Indonesia can help you navigate these interactions effectively and establish successful professional relationships. Here are some key aspects of meeting structure and protocol in Indonesian business culture:

Greetings and Introductions

- Begin the meeting by greeting your Indonesian counterparts with a handshake, using your right hand, as the left hand is considered impure. A light grip accompanied by a slight bow or nod of the head is customary.
- Address your counterparts using formal titles, such as "Pak" for men and "Ibu" for women, followed by their first name. This practice demonstrates respect for their position or seniority.
- In group settings, greet the most senior person first, followed by others in descending order of seniority. This demonstrates your respect for the hierarchy within the organization.

Meeting Agenda

- Providing an agenda ahead of the meeting is a good practice, as it allows your Indonesian counterparts to prepare for the discussion. However, be prepared for some flexibility in the agenda, as Indonesian business culture values adaptability and may deviate from the planned topics.
- Start the meeting with a brief overview of the agenda and the objectives of the meeting. This will help set the tone and ensure everyone is on the same page.

Decision-Making Process

- Decision-making in Indonesian business culture tends to be hierarchical, with authority centralized among senior executives or managers. Be prepared for decisions to be made at the top, and direct your proposals or suggestions to the appropriate person within the organization.

- Indonesian business culture values consensus-building, which can make the decision-making process slower than in some Western cultures. Be patient during this process and respect the need for consensus and harmony within the group.

Presentations and Visual Aids

- Use clear and concise visual aids or presentations to convey your ideas or proposals. Avoid using excessive text or overly complex visuals, as these may be distracting or difficult for your Indonesian counterparts to follow.

- Be prepared to provide translations or interpretations of your presentation materials, as not all participants may be fluent in English.

Negotiation and Closing

- Indonesian businesspeople may prefer to negotiate indirectly and diplomatically to maintain harmony and avoid confrontation. Be tactful and sensitive in your approach to negotiation and avoid being overly aggressive or confrontational.

- Be patient during the negotiation process and respect the need for consensus-building and consultation with others within the organization.

- Once an agreement has been reached, it's essential to follow up with a written summary or contract outlining the agreed-upon terms. This document should be carefully reviewed and signed by all relevant parties to ensure clarity and mutual understanding.

Tips for Effective Negotiation

Effective negotiation in Indonesian business culture requires understanding local customs, communication styles, and decision-making processes. Here are some tips to help you navigate negotiations successfully with your Indonesian counterparts:

Establish Personal Relationships

Personal relationships play a vital role in Indonesian business culture. Take the time to build trust and rapport with your Indonesian counterparts before delving into business negotiations. Small talk and informal conversations can help you establish a connection and set the foundation for successful negotiations.

Be Patient and Flexible

Patience and flexibility are key to successful negotiations in Indonesia. Decision-making processes can be slower than in some Western countries, as they often involve consensus-building and consultation with others in the organization. Be prepared to invest time in the negotiation process and adapt to changes in the schedule or agenda as they arise.

Understand Communication Styles

Indonesian communication tends to be indirect and diplomatic, with an emphasis on maintaining harmony and saving face. Be mindful of your tone and body language, and avoid being overly critical or confrontational in discussions. Pay attention to non-verbal cues, such as facial expressions or body language, which may indicate disagreement or discomfort.

Respect Hierarchy

Hierarchy is important in Indonesian business culture, and respecting the organizational structure is crucial during negotiations. Address your counterparts using formal titles, such as "Pak" for men and "Ibu" for women, followed by their first name. Direct your proposals or suggestions to the appropriate person within the organization, typically someone with decision-making authority.

Prepare Thoroughly

Before entering negotiations, ensure that you have a clear understanding of your goals, objectives, and limits. Be prepared to provide detailed information and supporting documentation to back up your proposals or requests. Demonstrating your expertise and thorough preparation can help build credibility with your Indonesian counterparts.

Use Diplomacy and Tact

Be diplomatic and tactful in your approach to negotiation, as Indonesian business culture values harmony and saving face. Avoid being overly aggressive or confrontational, and be prepared to compromise or make concessions to reach a mutually beneficial agreement.

Be Mindful of Cultural Sensitivities

Understanding Indonesian customs and cultural sensitivities can help you avoid misunderstandings or inadvertently causing offense during negotiations. Be respectful of religious practices, local customs, and social norms to demonstrate your commitment to fostering positive professional relationships.

Follow Up in Writing

Once an agreement has been reached, it's important to follow up with a written summary or contract outlining the agreed-upon terms. This document should be carefully reviewed and signed by all relevant parties to ensure clarity and mutual understanding.

Common Mistakes to Avoid

When conducting business meetings and negotiations in Indonesia, being aware of common mistakes and avoiding them can help you achieve better results and foster positive relationships with your Indonesian counterparts. Here are some common mistakes to avoid:

Ignoring Hierarchy

Not recognizing or respecting the hierarchical structure in Indonesian business culture can lead to misunderstandings or offense. Be aware of the organizational structure and ensure that you address and engage with the appropriate individuals, particularly those in decision-making positions.

Being Overly Direct or Confrontational

Indonesian communication styles tend to be more indirect and diplomatic. Avoid being overly direct, confrontational, or critical, as this may cause discomfort or offense. Instead, express your opinions or concerns tactfully and diplomatically to maintain harmony during negotiations.

Neglecting Relationship Building

Failing to invest time in building personal relationships with your Indonesian counterparts can hinder the negotiation process. Prioritize establishing trust and rapport before delving into business discussions, as strong personal connections can significantly influence decision-making in Indonesia.

Impatience

Being impatient or expecting quick decisions can be counterproductive in Indonesian business culture, where decision-making processes often involve consensus-building and consultation. Be patient and respect the time needed for thorough deliberation and discussion.

Disrespecting Local Customs and Norms

Not being aware of or respecting local customs, social norms, or religious practices can create barriers and misunderstandings during negotiations. Take the time to learn about Indonesian culture and ensure that you conduct yourself in a manner that is respectful and sensitive to local customs.

Inadequate Preparation

Entering negotiations without thorough preparation can undermine your credibility with your Indonesian counterparts. Be well-prepared and able to provide detailed information, supporting documentation, and clear proposals to demonstrate your professionalism and commitment.

Focusing Solely on Price

Focusing exclusively on price during negotiations can be limiting, as Indonesian businesspeople may value other factors, such as relationship building, service quality, or long-term partnerships. Be open to considering a broader range of factors when negotiating, and be prepared to make concessions in areas other than price to reach a mutually beneficial agreement.

Not Following Up in Writing

Failing to follow up with a written summary or contract after reaching an agreement can lead to confusion or misinterpretation of the agreed-upon terms. Ensure that you provide a clear and comprehensive written document outlining the terms of the agreement, and have it reviewed and signed by all relevant parties.

9. BUSINESS DINING AND ENTERTAINMENT

Traditional Hospitality

Traditional hospitality plays a significant role in Indonesian business culture, with dining and entertainment often used as a means to strengthen relationships and facilitate discussions in a more relaxed environment. Understanding the customs and practices associated with traditional hospitality in Indonesia can help you navigate these interactions effectively and build rapport with your Indonesian counterparts. Here are some key aspects of traditional hospitality in Indonesia:

Importance of Hospitality

Hospitality is highly valued in Indonesian culture, and your hosts may go to great lengths to make you feel welcome and comfortable. Accepting their invitations to dine or attend social events can help you build trust and establish stronger personal connections, which are crucial for successful business relationships in Indonesia.

Invitation Etiquette

When invited to a meal or event, it is polite to respond promptly and confirm your attendance. If you are unable to attend, inform your hosts as soon as possible and provide a valid reason for your absence. If you must decline an invitation, do so graciously and diplomatically to avoid causing offense.

Dining and Social Events

Business dining in Indonesia can take many forms, from informal meals at local eateries to more elaborate events at upscale restaurants or private homes. Be prepared to experience a wide range of Indonesian cuisine, which can vary significantly between regions. It is customary for hosts to order a variety of dishes to be shared among the group, so be open to trying new flavours and textures.

Table Manners

- When dining with Indonesian counterparts, wait for your host to begin eating or invite you to start before you begin eating.
- Use your right hand when eating or passing dishes, as the left hand is considered impure in Indonesian culture.

- Try to sample a little of each dish offered, as this demonstrates your appreciation and respect for the host's efforts.

Engaging in Conversation

During the meal or social event, engage in conversation with your Indonesian counterparts, focusing on light and non-controversial topics. Avoid discussing sensitive political or religious issues, and instead, opt for topics such as family, travel, or local culture. This is a valuable opportunity to learn more about your counterparts and build rapport outside of the formal business setting.

Toasts and Drinking Culture

Toasts are not a common practice in Indonesia, but if a toast is proposed, it is usually done with non-alcoholic beverages. Although alcohol is available in some establishments, it is important to be sensitive to the religious beliefs of your hosts and avoid consuming alcohol if they abstain due to their faith.

Expressing Gratitude

At the end of the meal or event, express your gratitude to your hosts for their hospitality and the opportunity to share the experience with them. A sincere and heartfelt expression of appreciation can help strengthen the bonds between you and your Indonesian counterparts.

By understanding and respecting the customs associated with traditional hospitality in Indonesia, you can foster stronger connections and rapport with your Indonesian colleagues and partners. Embrace these opportunities to engage in social and cultural exchanges, and enjoy the rich experiences that Indonesian hospitality has to offer.

10. LEISURE, ENTERTAINMENT AND FAMILY ACTIVITIES

Exploring Natural Wonders

Indonesia, an archipelago of over 17,000 islands, is home to an incredible array of natural wonders. From pristine beaches and lush rainforests to active volcanoes and unique wildlife, Indonesia offers a wealth of opportunities for travelers seeking to explore the country's diverse landscapes and ecosystems. Here are some must-see natural wonders in Indonesia:

Komodo National Park

Located in East Nusa Tenggara, **Komodo National Park** is home to the famous Komodo dragons, the world's largest lizard species. Spread across three main islands – Komodo, Rinca, and Padar – the park also boasts stunning beaches, vibrant coral reefs, and unique terrestrial fauna. Visitors can take guided tours to spot Komodo dragons in their natural habitat, go snorkelling or diving to explore the rich marine life, or trek through the park to enjoy panoramic views of the surrounding islands.

Raja Ampat Islands

Raja Ampat, situated in West Papua, is an archipelago consisting of over 1,500 small islands and islets. Known for its extraordinary marine biodiversity, Raja Ampat is a paradise for divers and snorkelers, with thousands of fish species, coral reefs, and other marine creatures. The islands also offer stunning landscapes, pristine beaches, and opportunities for birdwatching, trekking, and kayaking.

Mount Bromo

Mount Bromo, located in East Java, is an active volcano and part of the **Bromo Tengger Semeru National Park**. Its otherworldly landscape, with vast, barren volcanic plains and striking views of surrounding peaks, attracts thousands of tourists each year. Adventurous travellers can hike or ride a horse to the volcano's crater rim to witness the awe-inspiring sunrise or explore the nearby "Sea of Sand" and the Tengger Caldera.

Bali's Rice Terraces

The iconic rice terraces of Bali, particularly in Ubud and Jatiluwih, are a testament to the island's rich agricultural heritage. These UNESCO World Heritage-listed landscapes feature centuries-old, intricate systems of terraced rice paddies, sculpted into the hillsides and maintained by local communities. Visitors can take guided tours through the rice terraces, learn about traditional Balinese farming methods, and enjoy the stunning views of lush green fields.

Lake Toba

Situated in North Sumatra, **Lake Toba** is the largest volcanic lake in the world, formed by a massive eruption around 74,000 years ago. The lake's crystal-clear waters and the surrounding lush hills make it a popular destination for relaxation, swimming, and exploring local Batak culture. The central island of Samosir, home to traditional **Batak** villages and ancient stone monuments, offers opportunities for trekking, cycling, and cultural immersion.

Toraja Highlands

Located in South Sulawesi, the Toraja Highlands are known for their unique culture, breathtaking landscapes, and ancient burial sites. **Traditional Toraja** villages, with their distinctive boat-shaped houses, are nestled among terraced rice fields, limestone cliffs, and bamboo forests. Visitors can attend traditional ceremonies, explore ancient burial sites, and trek through the picturesque countryside, while learning about the Toraja people's customs and way of life.

Borneo's Rainforests

The island of Borneo, shared by Indonesia, Malaysia, and Brunei, is home to some of the world's oldest and most biodiverse rainforests. The Indonesian region of Kalimantan offers opportunities for eco-tourism, wildlife spotting, and cultural experiences with local Dayak tribes. Highlights include the **Tanjung Puting National Park**, where visitors can spot orangutans in their natural habitat, and the **Derawan Islands**, which boast beautiful beaches and vibrant coral reefs for snorkeling and diving.

Ijen Crater

Ijen Crater, also known as Kawah Ijen, is located in East Java and is famous for its striking turquoise-coloured acidic lake and blue sulphur flames. Visitors can hike up the volcano at night to witness the mesmerizing blue fire phenomenon and then continue to the crater rim to watch the sunrise over the stunning landscape. The Ijen Crater is also home to a unique sulphur mining operation, where local miners extract the mineral by hand in challenging conditions.

Wakatobi National Park

Wakatobi National Park, situated in Southeast Sulawesi, is a marine paradise known for its pristine coral reefs and diverse marine life. The park encompasses the four main islands of Wangi-Wangi, Kaledupa, Tomia, and Binongko, as well as numerous smaller islands and islets. Visitors can enjoy snorkelling, diving, and exploring the islands' white-sand beaches, mangrove forests, and traditional **Bajo villages**.

Lorentz National Park

Lorentz National Park, located in Papua, is the largest protected area in Southeast Asia and a UNESCO World Heritage site. The park encompasses a variety of ecosystems, from coastal mangroves and lowland rainforests to alpine tundra and glaciers. The park's diverse flora and fauna, including numerous endemic species, make it an exceptional destination for nature enthusiasts. Visitors can embark on multi-day treks through the park, explore the vast wilderness, and encounter local tribes living in harmony with their environment.

Historic Sites and Cultural Attractions

Indonesia's rich cultural heritage and history are reflected in its numerous historic sites and cultural attractions. From ancient temples and palaces to traditional villages and museums, these sites offer visitors a fascinating glimpse into the country's diverse past and vibrant traditions. Here are some must-visit historic sites and cultural attractions in Indonesia:

Borobudur Temple

Located in Central Java, **Borobudur** is the world's largest Buddhist temple and a UNESCO World Heritage site. Built in the 9th century, this magnificent monument features intricate stone carvings depicting the life of Buddha and the principles of Buddhism. Visitors can explore the temple's terraces, stupas, and galleries, while enjoying panoramic views of the surrounding landscape.

Prambanan Temple

Prambanan, another UNESCO World Heritage site, is a 9th-century Hindu temple complex in Central Java. Dedicated to the Hindu trinity of Brahma, Vishnu, and Shiva, Prambanan boasts impressive stone architecture and intricate carvings depicting scenes from the Ramayana epic. The temple complex also hosts traditional dance performances, such as the Ramayana ballet, which can be enjoyed under the stars.

Taman Sari Water Castle

Taman Sari, located in Yogyakarta, is a historic royal garden and former palace complex built in the 18th century by the Sultan of Yogyakarta. Featuring a unique blend of Javanese and European architectural styles, Taman Sari includes bathing pools, ornate pavilions, and underground tunnels. Visitors can explore the complex and learn about the history and culture of the Yogyakarta Sultanate.

Uluwatu Temple

Perched on a cliff overlooking the Indian Ocean in Bali, <u>Uluwatu Temple</u> is a stunning Balinese Hindu temple dating back to the 11th century. The temple is dedicated to the deity of the sea and is one of Bali's most sacred sites. Visitors can enjoy the spectacular views, watch traditional <u>**Kecak dance**</u> performances at sunset, and encounter the mischievous monkeys that inhabit the temple grounds.

Fort Rotterdam

<u>Fort Rotterdam</u>, located in Makassar, South Sulawesi, is a well-preserved Dutch colonial fortress dating back to the 17th century. The fort now houses a museum displaying artifacts from the region's pre-colonial and colonial history, as well as traditional arts and crafts. Visitors can explore the fort's bastions, barracks, and gardens while learning about the history of the <u>**Dutch East India Company**</u> and the spice trade in Indonesia.

Tana Toraja

<u>Tana Toraja</u>, situated in the highlands of South Sulawesi, is renowned for its unique culture, architecture, and ancient burial sites. Traditional Toraja villages feature distinctive boat-shaped houses, known as <u>**tongkonan**</u>, and elaborately carved wooden grave sites. Visitors can attend traditional ceremonies, explore ancient burial sites, and learn about the Toraja people's customs and beliefs surrounding life, death, and the afterlife.

Pura Besakih

<u>Pura Besakih</u>, also known as the Mother Temple, is the most important and largest Hindu temple complex in Bali. Located on the slopes of <u>**Mount Agung**</u>, the temple consists of 23 separate temples and numerous shrines dedicated to various Hindu deities. Pura Besakih is an important pilgrimage site for Balinese Hindus and hosts several major religious ceremonies throughout the year.

Museum Nasional Indonesia

The <u>**National Museum of Indonesia**</u>, located in Jakarta, is the country's premier museum, showcasing Indonesia's rich history, cultural diversity, and archaeological treasures. The museum's extensive collections include prehistoric artifacts, Hindu-Buddhist sculptures, traditional textiles, Islamic art, and contemporary art. Visitors can explore the museum's many galleries, attend special exhibitions and events, and learn about the history and culture of Indonesia.

Wayang Museum

The **Wayang Museum**, also in Jakarta, is dedicated to wayang, the traditional Indonesian art of shadow puppetry. The museum houses an extensive collection of wayang puppets from across Indonesia, as well as traditional gamelan instruments and other cultural artifacts. Visitors can watch puppet performances, learn about the history and technique of wayang, and even try their hand at making their own puppets.

Bali Aga Villages

Bali Aga villages, located in several areas in Bali, are traditional villages inhabited by the original Balinese people, who have preserved their unique culture and customs for centuries. The villages feature traditional architecture, arts and crafts, and ceremonies, including the famous **Ngaben cremation ceremony**. Visitors can learn about the Bali Aga way of life and participate in cultural activities such as weaving, cooking, and dance.

Family-Friendly Activities and Entertainment

Indonesia offers a wealth of family-friendly activities and entertainment options for travelers of all ages. From theme parks and water parks to wildlife parks and cultural experiences, there's something for everyone. Here are some of the best family-friendly activities and entertainment options in Indonesia:

Waterbom Bali

Waterbom Bali, located in Kuta, is a water park that features over 20 thrilling water rides and attractions for all ages. From lazy rivers and wave pools to high-speed water slides and a flow rider, Waterbom Bali is a popular destination for families seeking fun in the sun.

Bali Safari and Marine Park

Bali Safari and Marine Park, located in Gianyar, is a wildlife park that offers a unique safari experience, with over 100 species of animals from around the world, including elephants, tigers, and orangutans. Visitors can also enjoy animal shows, safari rides, and water park attractions.

Trans Studio Bandung

Trans Studio Bandung, located in West Java, is an indoor theme park that features a variety of rides and attractions, including roller coasters, virtual reality experiences, and interactive games. The park also includes a shopping mall and food court.

Taman Mini Indonesia Indah

<u>Taman Mini Indonesia Indah</u>, located in Jakarta, is a cultural theme park that showcases Indonesia's rich cultural diversity and history. The park features traditional architecture, arts and crafts, and performances from across Indonesia's many regions.

Monkey Forest Ubud

The <u>Monkey Forest in Ubud</u>, Bali, is a nature reserve and temple complex that is home to over 600 long-tailed macaque monkeys. Visitors can observe the monkeys in their natural habitat, walk through the forest and enjoy the beautiful scenery, and explore the temple complex.

Jatim Park

<u>Jatim Park</u>, located in East Java, is a family-friendly theme park that features a range of attractions, from roller coasters and water rides to science exhibits and a dinosaur park. The park also includes a zoo and botanical gardens.

Kampung Sampireun

Kampung Sampireun, located in Garut, West Java, is a traditional village resort that offers a unique cultural experience for families. Visitors can stay in traditional Javanese-style bungalows, enjoy traditional food and entertainment, and participate in activities such as traditional weaving, fishing, and bamboo rafting.

Kampung Gajah Wonderland

Kampung Gajah Wonderland, located in Bandung, is a family-friendly attraction that features a range of activities and attractions, including an amusement park, water park, petting zoo, and outdoor adventure activities.

Museum Angkut

<u>Museum Angkut</u>, located in Batu, East Java, is a transportation museum that showcases a wide variety of vehicles from different eras and cultures, from vintage cars and motorcycles to planes and trains. The museum also includes a 3D cinema and a food court.

Legoland Malaysia

While not located in Indonesia, Legoland Malaysia, located just across the border from Indonesia in Johor Bahru, is a popular destination for families from Indonesia. The theme park features Lego-themed rides and attractions, including roller coasters, water rides, and miniature Lego replicas of famous landmarks.

Celebrations and Festivals

Indonesian traditions are often celebrated through various festivals and events throughout the year. From religious celebrations to cultural festivals, Indonesia's festivals offer visitors a unique insight into the country's diverse cultural heritage. Here are some of the most popular celebrations and festivals in Indonesia:

Nyepi

Nyepi is the Balinese Day of Silence, which marks the Hindu New Year. This day is celebrated by a day of complete silence, fasting, and meditation. Balinese people believe that this day should be a time of introspection, and that it helps to cleanse the island of negative influences.

Galungan and Kuningan

Galungan and Kuningan are two important Hindu festivals celebrated in Bali. The festivals mark the victory of good over evil, and the ancestors are believed to return to the earth during this time. The festivities include temple ceremonies, offerings of food and flowers, and traditional dance performances.

Jakarta Fair

The Jakarta Fair is an annual event held in Jakarta, which attracts millions of visitors every year. The fair showcases Indonesian products, services, and cultural performances. There are also carnival rides, games, and food stalls.

Lebaran

Lebaran, also known as Eid al-Fitr, is the biggest Muslim holiday in Indonesia. It marks the end of Ramadan, the month of fasting. Lebaran is celebrated by a feast with family and friends, and Muslims traditionally give money or gifts to children.

Cap Go Meh

Cap Go Meh is a Chinese-Indonesian festival celebrated on the 15th day of the Lunar New Year. The festival includes parades, lion and dragon dances, and traditional food offerings.

Toraja Funeral Ceremonies

Toraja Funeral Ceremonies are unique cultural events held in the highlands of South Sulawesi. The ceremonies are elaborate and last for several days, during which time the deceased is laid to rest in a carved wooden coffin, which is placed in a cave or hung from a cliff. The ceremonies include traditional dances, animal sacrifices, and offerings of food and drink.

Jakarta International Java Jazz Festival

The **Jakarta International Java Jazz Festival** is one of the biggest jazz festivals in the world, attracting thousands of jazz enthusiasts from around the globe. The festival features performances by local and international jazz musicians, and includes workshops and clinics for jazz musicians.

Bali Arts Festival

The **Bali Arts Festival** is an annual event held in Bali, which showcases traditional Balinese art and culture. The festival includes traditional dance and music performances, handicraft exhibitions, and culinary events.

Waisak

Waisak is an important Buddhist festival celebrated in Indonesia, which marks the birth, enlightenment, and death of Buddha. The festival is celebrated with processions, offerings of food and flowers, and traditional dances.

Krakatoa Festival

The Krakatoa Festival is an annual event held in Lampung, which celebrates the natural beauty of the area and the famous Krakatoa volcano. The festival includes traditional music and dance performances, cultural exhibitions, and culinary events.

11. PRACTICAL TIPS FOR TRAVELLERS AND EXPATS

Safety and Security Tips

Indonesia can be a safe and enjoyable place to live as an expat, but it's important to be aware of potential safety and security risks. As with any foreign country, it's important to take necessary precautions to ensure your safety and security. Here are some safety and security tips for expats in Indonesia:

Be aware of your surroundings

It's important to be aware of your surroundings at all times, especially in crowded or unfamiliar areas. Avoid walking alone at night, and stay in well-lit areas with other people around.

Use reliable transportation

Use reliable and trusted transportation options, such as taxis or ride-sharing services, to get around. Avoid using unlicensed or informal modes of transportation, such as motorcycle taxis or public buses, as these can be less safe and less reliable.

Keep valuables out of sight

Keep your valuables out of sight when in public, and avoid carrying large amounts of cash or expensive jewellery. Use a money belt or secure bag to keep your important documents and money safe.

Be cautious of scams and pickpocketing

Be cautious of scams and pickpocketing, especially in crowded areas such as markets and tourist attractions. Keep your belongings close to you and avoid leaving them unattended.

Be prepared for natural disasters

Indonesia is prone to natural disasters such as earthquakes, tsunamis, and volcanic eruptions. It's important to be prepared for these events by keeping emergency supplies on hand and knowing evacuation routes and procedures.

Stay up to date on security alerts

Stay up to date on security alerts and travel advisories issued by your embassy or consulate. These alerts can provide valuable information on potential security risks and safety concerns in specific areas.

Respect local customs and laws

Respect local customs and laws to avoid any potential conflicts or misunderstandings. Be aware of any restrictions on dress, behaviour, or alcohol consumption in certain areas.

Stay connected with other expats and local community

Stay connected with other expats and the local community for support and information on living safely in Indonesia. Joining expat groups or online forums can be a great way to meet other expats and learn from their experiences.

Healthcare and insurance

As an expat living in Indonesia, healthcare and insurance are important considerations. Indonesia has both public and private healthcare systems, and it's important to understand the options available to you as an expat. Here are some tips for expats on healthcare and insurance in Indonesia:

Healthcare:

- Private healthcare in Indonesia can offer better quality care and shorter wait times than the public system. Many private hospitals and clinics in Indonesia are equipped with modern facilities and staffed by trained professionals.
- Research your healthcare options before you arrive in Indonesia, including the location and quality of nearby hospitals and clinics. Consider factors such as the availability of English-speaking doctors and the cost of medical care.
- Take preventative measures to maintain your health, such as practicing good hygiene and getting recommended vaccinations. Be aware of common health risks in Indonesia, such as mosquito-borne diseases like dengue fever and malaria.
- Prepare for emergencies by knowing the location of the nearest hospital and emergency services. Keep a list of important emergency contacts and carry a copy of your medical records with you.

Insurance:

- Consider purchasing international health insurance that covers medical expenses and emergencies while you're living in Indonesia. Make sure the policy covers the specific medical treatments and procedures that you may need.

- Research local insurance options in Indonesia, including those offered by private healthcare providers. Some employers may also provide health insurance coverage as part of their benefits package.
- Check the coverage limits and exclusions of any insurance policy before purchasing. Make sure you understand the terms and conditions of the policy and the claims process.
- Keep your insurance documents with you at all times, including your policy number and emergency contact information. Make sure you know how to contact your insurance provider in case of an emergency.

12. OVERCOMING STEREOTYPES AND PREJUDICES

Common Misconceptions and Stereotypes

Indonesia is a country with a rich culture and diverse population, but there are still many misconceptions and stereotypes that exist about the country and its people. Here are some of the most common misconceptions and stereotypes about Indonesia:

Indonesia is a dangerous country

While Indonesia has had its share of natural disasters and security issues, the country is generally safe for tourists and expats. As with any foreign country, it's important to be aware of your surroundings and take necessary precautions to ensure your safety.

All Indonesians are Muslim

While Indonesia has the largest Muslim population in the world, not all Indonesians are Muslim. There are also significant Christian, Hindu, and Buddhist populations in the country.

Indonesia is a poor country

While Indonesia is still considered a developing country, the economy has been growing rapidly in recent years. The country has a large middle class and a growing consumer market, making it an attractive destination for businesses and investors.

Indonesians are not educated

Indonesia has a large and well-educated population, with a literacy rate of over 95%. The country has several highly-ranked universities and many Indonesians pursue higher education both in Indonesia and abroad.

Indonesian cuisine is spicy

While some Indonesian dishes are spicy, not all of them are. Indonesian cuisine is diverse and includes a wide range of flavours and spices, depending on the region and the dish.

Bali is representative of Indonesia

While Bali is a popular destination for tourists, it's important to remember that it's just one small part of Indonesia. There are many other regions in the country that offer unique cultures, traditions, and attractions.

Indonesians are reserved and shy

While Indonesians may be more reserved than people from some Western cultures, they are generally friendly and welcoming. Indonesians value hospitality and are often eager to engage with foreigners.

Strategies for overcoming biases and promoting understanding

As with any foreign country, it's important to approach Indonesia with an open mind and a willingness to learn about its culture and people. Here are some strategies for overcoming biases and promoting understanding in Indonesia:

Learn about the culture and history

Learn about the culture and history of Indonesia before visiting or living in the country. This can help you gain a better understanding of the customs, traditions, and beliefs of its people.

Engage with the local community

Engage with the local community to learn about their daily lives, customs, and traditions. This can help you develop a deeper appreciation and understanding of their culture.

Avoid stereotypes and assumptions

Avoid making assumptions or generalizations about the people or culture of Indonesia. Recognize that diversity exists within the country and that each individual has their own unique experiences and perspectives.

Be respectful and open-minded

Be respectful and open-minded when interacting with Indonesians. Show interest in their culture and traditions and avoid imposing your own beliefs or values.

Learn the language

Learn some basic Indonesian phrases to help you communicate with the local community. This can help you build rapport and establish a deeper connection with the people.

Participate in cultural activities

Participate in cultural activities such as festivals and ceremonies to learn more about the customs and traditions of the local community. This can also help you build relationships and connect with others.

Seek out diverse perspectives

Seek out diverse perspectives on Indonesia and its culture, including those of different ethnic groups and social classes. This can help you gain a more nuanced and comprehensive understanding of the country and its people.

13. BUILDING CROSS-CULTURAL RELATIONSHIPS

Effective Communication and Conflict Resolution

Effective communication and conflict resolution are key components of building cross-cultural relationships in Indonesia. Here are some tips for expats on effective communication and conflict resolution in Indonesia:

Learn the language

Learning some basic Indonesian phrases can help you communicate more effectively with the local community. This can help you establish rapport and build relationships with Indonesians.

Be aware of nonverbal cues

Be aware of nonverbal cues such as body language and tone of voice, which can vary depending on the culture. Indonesians may use indirect communication and nonverbal cues to express their thoughts and feelings, so it's important to be sensitive to these cues.

Listen actively

Active listening is an important part of effective communication. Take the time to listen to the perspectives and concerns of Indonesians and show that you understand and value their opinions.

Be respectful

Be respectful of the culture and traditions of Indonesians. Show interest and respect for their beliefs and customs, and avoid imposing your own values or beliefs.

Avoid confrontation

Indonesians may avoid confrontation or direct conflict, preferring instead to use indirect communication and negotiation. Be mindful of this and avoid being confrontational in your communication style.

Seek to understand

Seek to understand the perspective and context of Indonesians in any conflict or disagreement. This can help you find common ground and work towards a mutually acceptable solution.

Be patient

Building cross-cultural relationships takes time and patience. Be patient in your communication and conflict resolution, and be willing to compromise and find creative solutions.

Adapting to cultural differences

Adapting to cultural differences is an important part of living as an expat in Indonesia. Here are some tips for expats on how to adapt to cultural differences in Indonesia:

Learn about the culture

Learn about the culture and customs of Indonesia before you arrive. This can help you understand the social norms, values, and beliefs of Indonesians.

Respect local customs

Respect local customs and traditions, even if they are different from what you are used to. Show interest in the culture and be willing to learn and adapt.

Develop relationships

Develop relationships with Indonesians, whether it's with colleagues, neighbours, or friends. This can help you gain a better understanding of the culture and develop a support network.

Learn the language

Learning some basic Indonesian phrases can help you communicate more effectively with Indonesians and show that you respect their culture.

Be patient

Be patient and understanding of cultural differences. Indonesians may have a different sense of time, communication style, and decision-making process than what you are used to.

Be flexible

Be flexible and adaptable in your approach to work and socializing. Indonesians may have different work and social customs, so be willing to adjust your expectations and approach.

Embrace new experiences

Embrace new experiences and try new things, such as trying local food, attending cultural events, or visiting new places. This can help you appreciate and enjoy the unique aspects of Indonesian culture.

Developing empathy and cultural intelligence

Developing empathy and cultural intelligence is essential for fostering meaningful cross-cultural relationships, both personally and professionally. In this chapter, we will discuss strategies and tips for cultivating empathy and cultural intelligence to better connect with people from different backgrounds.

Educate yourself about different cultures.

Invest time in learning about the values, customs, and traditions of various cultures, especially those you frequently interact with. Understanding cultural nuances can help you appreciate their perspectives and anticipate potential communication challenges.

Engage in active listening.

Make a conscious effort to listen attentively to others, without interrupting or imposing your own opinions. Active listening can help you gain deeper insights into their experiences, feelings, and perspectives, which is crucial for developing empathy.

Practice perspective-taking.

Put yourself in the shoes of others and try to understand their thoughts, emotions, and experiences from their point of view. This can help you appreciate the challenges they face and foster empathy and understanding.

Develop emotional intelligence.

Emotional intelligence refers to the ability to recognize, understand, and manage your own emotions and the emotions of others. Enhancing your emotional intelligence can help you better understand the emotional underpinnings of cross-cultural interactions and respond more empathetically.

Be curious and open-minded.

Approach cultural differences with curiosity and an open mind. Ask questions and seek to learn more about the experiences and perspectives of others, without judgment or preconceived notions.

Observe and reflect on cultural interactions.

Pay close attention to how you and others respond to cultural differences in various contexts. Reflect on these interactions to identify areas where you can improve your empathy and cultural intelligence.

Seek diverse experiences and relationships.

Expose yourself to diverse experiences and relationships by interacting with people from different cultural backgrounds. These experiences can help you develop a broader understanding of the world and enhance your empathy and cultural intelligence.

Foster a growth mindset.

Embrace a growth mindset, which involves viewing challenges as opportunities for learning and growth. This mindset can help you approach cultural differences with a willingness to learn and adapt, rather than feeling threatened or overwhelmed.

Participate in cultural training and workshops.

Consider attending workshops or participating in cultural training programs to enhance your understanding of different cultures and develop your empathy and cultural intelligence.

Continuously learn and adapt.

Recognize that developing empathy and cultural intelligence is an ongoing process that requires continuous learning, reflection, and adaptation. Stay committed to personal growth and be open to feedback and new experiences.

14. CASE STUDIES AND REAL LIFE EXAMPLES

Stories and anecdotes illustrating cultural challenges and successes

Expats living in Indonesia often experience a myriad of cultural challenges and successes. By sharing their stories and anecdotes, they provide valuable insights into navigating Indonesian culture, fostering understanding, and promoting cultural exchange. Here are a few examples:

Language Barrier and Success

John, an American expat, struggled with the Indonesian language upon arriving in Jakarta. Determined to improve, he enrolled in a Bahasa Indonesia language course. One day, he stumbled upon a group of locals playing a street soccer game. Despite his limited language skills, he managed to ask if he could join them. The locals welcomed him enthusiastically, and through this experience, John not only improved his language skills but also made lasting friendships.

The Importance of Respecting Local Customs

A British expat named Sarah found herself in a small Javanese village, where she was invited to attend a traditional wedding ceremony. Unaware of local customs, she wore a short dress, which was considered inappropriate attire for the occasion. Realizing her mistake, Sarah quickly apologized and borrowed a traditional batik sarong from her host. This experience taught her the importance of understanding and respecting local customs to avoid unintentional offense.

The Generosity of Indonesian People

David, an Australian expat, was working in Bali when he lost his wallet containing his cash and identification. Distraught, he mentioned his predicament to a local food vendor, who insisted on treating him to a meal and offering him a place to stay for the night. The next day, the vendor helped David contact the necessary authorities to resolve his situation. This act of kindness left a lasting impression on David, who came to appreciate the generosity and warmth of the Indonesian people.

Adjusting to a Different Pace of Life

Maria, a Spanish expat, initially found it challenging to adapt to the slower pace of life in Indonesia. After several months, she learned to embrace the "jam karet" or "rubber time" mentality and found a newfound appreciation for the importance of taking time to relax and connect with others.

Embracing Indonesian Cuisine

Tom, a Canadian expat, was initially hesitant to try Indonesian street food due to concerns about hygiene. One day, he mustered the courage to try nasi goreng from a street vendor, and it turned out to be one of the best meals he had ever tasted. This experience led him to explore the rich and diverse Indonesian cuisine, and he soon became a regular at local food stalls.

Lessons learned and best practices

Living in Indonesia as an expat can be a rewarding and enriching experience. Expats often learn valuable lessons and develop best practices to make the most of their time in the country. Here are some key lessons learned and best practices for expats in Indonesia:

Learn the language

Though English is widely spoken in urban areas, learning Bahasa Indonesia, the official language, can greatly enhance your experience. It will not only help you communicate more effectively but also show respect for the local culture and foster deeper connections with locals.

Be culturally sensitive

It's essential to learn about local customs and traditions to avoid accidentally offending anyone. This includes understanding religious practices, social norms, and etiquette. For example, when visiting a mosque or temple, dress modestly and remove your shoes before entering.

Embrace the local cuisine

Indonesian cuisine is diverse, flavourful, and often inexpensive. Don't be afraid to try street food and local dishes, as they can provide an authentic taste of the culture. Be mindful of hygiene practices and opt for popular stalls with a high turnover to minimize the risk of foodborne illnesses.

Be prepared for "jam karet"

"Jam karet" or "rubber time" refers to the flexible and slower-paced approach to timekeeping in Indonesia. Patience is key, as appointments and schedules may not always run on time. Embrace this cultural difference and be prepared to adjust your expectations.

Build a support network

Connecting with other expats and locals can be an invaluable resource for navigating life in Indonesia. Seek out social groups, clubs, or online communities where you can share experiences, ask questions, and make new friends.

Stay informed about local laws and regulations

Ensure that you understand and adhere to local laws and regulations, such as visa requirements, taxation, and driving rules. Ignorance of the law is not an excuse, and failure to comply can result in fines or other penalties.

Be cautious with traffic

Traffic in Indonesia can be chaotic, especially in urban areas. Take the time to understand local driving habits, follow traffic rules, and be extra cautious while driving or crossing the street. Alternatively, consider using public transportation or ride-hailing services.

Prioritize your health and safety

Familiarize yourself with local healthcare facilities and emergency contact numbers. Also, take preventive measures against common health risks, such as mosquito-borne diseases, by using insect repellent and wearing appropriate clothing.

Be mindful of the environment

Respect the natural beauty of Indonesia by minimizing your environmental impact. Avoid littering, conserve water and energy, and support eco-friendly practices and businesses whenever possible.

Stay open-minded and adaptable

Lastly, maintain a positive attitude and be open to new experiences. Embrace the cultural differences, and you'll find your time in Indonesia to be a fulfilling and transformative experience.

Resources and Further Reading

Books, articles, and websites for further exploration

Books:

- "Culture Shock! Indonesia: A Survival Guide to Customs and Etiquette" by Cathie Draine and Barbara Hall
- "Indonesia, Etc.: Exploring the Improbable Nation" by Elizabeth Pisani
- "The Year of Living Dangerously" by Christopher J. Koch
- "A House in Bali" by Colin McPhee
- "Eat, Pray, Love" by Elizabeth Gilbert

Articles:

- "10 Tips for Living in Indonesia" - Expatriate Health Insurance (https://www.expatexchange.com/ctryguide/4577/89/Indonesia/Expats-in-Indonesia-10-Tips-for-Living-in-Indonesia)

- "The Ultimate Guide for Moving to Bali" - Bali Manual (https://www.balimanual.com/the-ultimate-guide-for-moving-to-bali/)
- "Living in Indonesia: A Guide for Expats" - Expat Guide Asia (https://www.expatguides.com/asia/indonesia/)

Websites & Blogs:

- Expat Indonesia Forum - A community for expats in Indonesia to share advice, ask questions, and discuss their experiences. (https://www.livinginindonesiaforum.org/)
- Indonesia Expat - An English-language magazine and website providing news, articles, and information for expats in Indonesia. (https://indonesiaexpat.id/)
- Bali Expat Forum - A community forum for expats living in Bali, Indonesia, to share advice and experiences. (https://balipod.com/)
- Jakarta 100 Bars - A nightlife guide and blog with information about Jakarta's bars, clubs, and restaurants. (https://www.jakarta100bars.com/)
- Discover Your Indonesia - A travel blog offering insights into Indonesian culture, destinations, and travel tips. (https://discoveryourindonesia.com/)

Language learning resources and cultural organisations

Language Learning Resources:

- Duolingo - A popular language learning app that offers a gamified approach to learning Indonesian. (https://www.duolingo.com/course/id/en/Learn-Indonesian)
- Pimsleur - An audio-based language learning program that offers Indonesian courses for beginners. (https://www.pimsleur.com/learn-indonesian)
- BahasaKita - A website providing lessons, vocabulary, grammar, and other resources for learning Indonesian. (https://www.bahasakita.com/)
- Transparent Language - A comprehensive language learning platform with an Indonesian course. (https://www.transparent.com/learn-indonesian/)
- italki - A platform where you can find professional Indonesian teachers for one-on-one online lessons. (https://www.italki.com/teachers/indonesian)
- Memrise - A language learning app that offers Indonesian courses and utilizes spaced repetition for effective learning. (https://www.memrise.com/courses/english/indonesian/)

Cultural Organizations:

- Indonesian Heritage Society - A non-profit organization that aims to promote interest in and knowledge of Indonesia's cultural heritage. They offer lectures, study groups, and cultural tours. (https://www.heritagejkt.org/)

- The Indonesian Cultural Center (Rumah Indonesia) - A cultural center in several countries that promote Indonesian culture and arts through events, workshops, and exhibitions. (http://indonesiaculturalcenter.com/)
- American Indonesian Cultural & Educational Foundation (AICEF) - A non-profit organization in the United States that aims to promote mutual understanding between Indonesia and the US through cultural, educational, and social programs. (http://aicef.us/)
- Indonesian Arts and Culture Scholarship (IACS) - A program organized by the Indonesian Ministry of Foreign Affairs that offers international participants the opportunity to learn Indonesian arts, culture, and language. (https://www.kemlu.go.id/portal/en/read/2326/halaman_list_lainnya/indonesian-arts-and-culture-scholarship)